The Creating CoPOWERment® Workbook

*Embracing the Power of
Positive Psychology, Healing Stories and Explorations
to Create the Life You Want*

Lani Kwon, MA

Copyright © 2013 Lani Kwon, MA

All rights reserved. No part of this book may be used or reproduced by any means, graphic, electronic, or mechanical, including photocopying, recording, taping or by any information storage retrieval system without the written permission of the publisher except in the case of brief quotations embodied in critical articles and reviews.

Balboa Press books may be ordered through booksellers or by contacting:

*Balboa Press
A Division of Hay House
1663 Liberty Drive
Bloomington, IN 47403
www.balboapress.com
1 (877) 407-4847*

Because of the dynamic nature of the Internet, any web addresses or links contained in this book may have changed since publication and may no longer be valid. The views expressed in this work are solely those of the author and do not necessarily reflect the views of the publisher, and the publisher hereby disclaims any responsibility for them.

The author of this book does not dispense medical advice or prescribe the use of any technique as a form of treatment for physical, emotional, or medical problems without the advice of a physician, either directly or indirectly. The intent of the author is only to offer information of a general nature to help you in your quest for emotional and spiritual well-being. In the event you use any of the information in this book for yourself, which is your constitutional right, the author and the publisher assume no responsibility for your actions.

Certain royalty-free licensed imagery © InMagine LLC

Printed in the United States of America.

*ISBN: 978-1-4525-7928-3 (sc)
ISBN: 978-1-4525-7930-6 (hc)
ISBN: 978-1-4525-7929-0 (e)*

Library of Congress Control Number: 2013914041

Balboa Press rev. date: 8/16/2013

*This book is dedicated to my son, Noa,
best friend and co-parent, Justin Meilgaard,
and to the Kwon-Hamada-Temple-Livingston
and Meilgaard-Meadows-Goodfellow-Rowland families.*

Author Biography

Lani Kwon, MA, Founder of the Creating CoPOWERment® Center LLC, provides clients with step-by-step tools and resources for life transformation and re-design. She has over two decades of experience in crisis counseling, teaching, public speaking and writing, and she combined these interests into a life coaching practice in Ann Arbor, Michigan in 2005. Now back home in Hawai'i, she offers Creating CoPOWERment® workshops for groups, presents larger presentations for companies and non-profit organizations, and provides online, teleconferencing and in-person one-on-one coaching worldwide. She serves and supports people going through many different types of life transitions: graduation, career change, identity crisis, coming out, moving, pregnancy, adoption, divorce, recovery, retirement, among others.

Lani is a Newfield Network Graduate Coach (2011-2012) http://www.newfieldnetwork.com and has been a member of the International Coach Federation http://www.coachfederation.org since 2006. She graduated Magna Cum Laude from Pearl City High School in 1987, the University of Hawai'i at Mānoa in 1991 with a BA in English with Honors and earned a Master's degree in English Literature with a Specialization in Creative Writing from the University of Colorado at Boulder in 1995. She participates in ongoing trainings and conferences internationally.

Lani is also an artist, writer and a mom. She lives with her son, Noa, in Honolulu.

Endorsements for
The Creating CoPOWERment® Workbook:

"*The Creating CoPOWERment® Workbook* is quite simply a calling: an invitation to your authentic self, to live your life with more meaning and joy. Lani writes elegantly as she shares many personal stories designed to give you insights and light your way. She acts as your guide as you journey deep within the tapestry of your life to find what makes you truly come alive. This is your life, and Lani's work will help you to build a life that really resonates."
–Jayne Warrilow, Author of *The Secret Language of Resonance*
www.resonantcoaching.com

"'You're not alone. Only you can do it.' Lani's *Creating CoPOWERment® Workbook* hinges on balancing personal responsibility with an awareness of interdependence. Nobody can build the life of your dreams for you, and, at the same time, your dream life needs to be constructed in harmony with others. Lani has done the hard work of filtering out what works. Follow your own inner knowing with this skillful guide."
–Clayton Gibson, Founder of MyOutSpirit.com and Author of *Shirt of Flame: The Secret Gay Art of War*
www.MyOutSpirit.com

"I resonate with Lani Kwon's *Creating CoPOWERment® Workbook* which is living: creating meaning, more self-love and joy. The stories she shares of her own and others' experiences of transition allow the reader to discover why this process is important and how change and growth are possible. I LOVE

that she starts the book with awareness, as this is where all life begins. The exercises are simple and powerful."
–Mary Anne Flanagan, Toning the OM®
www.ToningtheOm.com

"We are often brainwashed by society and the media into thinking that we have to be successful and have no problems, else we are failures. In Lani's wonderful *Creating CoPOWERment® Workbook*, she reminds us of the downside of holding it all in and pretending it doesn't exist, as well as the upside of examining our issues and coming to terms with them. When you read this book and do the exercises, you will move closer to showing up in the world as your Authentic Self, and accept the flawed, imperfect and glorious human being that is you! That, in my opinion, is the most direct path to real and lasting Happiness."
–Jim Smith, PCC, author of *Happiness at the Speed of Life*
www.TheExecutiveHappinessCoach.com

"Lani's years of offering Creating CoPOWERment® workshops have yielded a profound understanding of how we support and encourage one another in our personal growth. Lani has been successful in distilling her experiences into a readable and inspiring workbook. She includes compelling examples from her personal experiences that inspire the reader to embark on her own journey within."
–Patricia Fero, LMSW, author of *Mining for Diamonds*, *What Happens When Women Wake Up* and *Sacred Marching Orders: Igniting the Solar Feminine at the Dawn of a New Age*
www.patriciaferolifecoach.com

"From the moment we open our eyes in 'Awareness,' the first chapter of *The Creating CoPOWERment® Workbook*, Lani takes us on a journey through stories and practical exercises

that empower us towards 'Becoming a Parent,' giving birth to the life we are meant to live. The life stories and lessons shared are compelling and motivate us forward into tangible exercises, which support us on the path of opening our minds, hearts, and deeper self-realization. The sensual sensibility of 'being' human flows dynamically throughout the workbook and challenges us to do the same. Lani's gift for delivering this message and gracefully offering guidance along the way is sustainable and a propelling core value in the spirit of enlightenment."
–Master Wasentha Young, Director of the Peaceful Dragon School
www.PeacefulDragonSchool.com

"Lani is an amazingly inspiring and compassionate coach. She has an incredible drive to help her clients through the transitions of life. You can always be assured that Lani will be fully present, committing all of her energy to what she co-creates with her clients so that every action and interaction is maximized. Lani's dedicated work on *The Creating CoPOWERment® Workbook* is another testament to her passion and determination to serve."
–Karen Davis, Executive and Personal Coach, Karen Davis Coaching
www.KarenDavisCoaching.com

"One of the most interesting disconnects in we humans is the degree to which we admire wisdom and yet lack methodologies and practices to learn wisdom. In effect our strategy is to *hope wisdom finds us.* Lani's workbook fills this gap practically and simply. The question isn't *Do I have wisdom?* but rather *Do I have wisdom available?* I see the work offered in Lani's workbook to be a practical course in developing our access to

our own wisdom. Do you have the wisdom to take up wisdom as a practice?"
–Dan Newby, Senior Course Leader, Newfield Network
www.newfieldnetwork.com

"…In my thirty years as a coach, I have learned that embracing the power of satisfaction, gratitude and the act of serving others are essential aspects in living a good life. You can never truly be yourself without the joy of serving others. You can never be satisfied without connecting with otherness and living with gratitude. In spite of the powerful cultural forces that predicate dissatisfaction as an economic engine, there is a deep part of your soul that knows differently. That part of you knows the essence of gratitude and the magic of living a meaningful life. We must recover the sacredness in our daily lives. We must recover our sense of connectivity with one another and nature. Read Lani's book. There you will find a sweet invitation.
–Julio Olalla, Founder of Newfield Network
www.newfieldnetwork.com

Works Reprinted by Permission

Grateful acknowledgment and aloha to the following writers, editors and publishers whose research, writing and work have inspired me and informed this book. Fair use permissions granted, public domain and/or reprinted with permission of the publisher(s), editor(s) and/or author(s) as indicated below:

Reprinted with permission of the publisher. From *Something More: Excavating Your Authentic Self* ©1998 by Sarah Ban Breathnach, Grand Central Publishing, New York, NY. All rights reserved. http://www.hachettebookgroup.com.

Reprinted with permission of the publisher. From *Daring Greatly: How the Courage to Be Vulnerable Transforms the Way We Live, Love, Parent and Lead* ©2012 by Brené Brown, Ph.D., LMSW, Gotham Books, a member of Penguin Group (USA) Inc., New York, NY. All rights reserved. www.us.penguingroup.com.

Reprinted fair use and with permission of the author. From "Your Body Language Shapes Who You Are," ©2012 by Professor Amy Cuddy, Ph.D., TED Global, June 2012. Posted October 2012. Researched 20 May 2013. All rights reserved. http://www.ted.com/talks/amy_cuddy_your_body_language_shapes_who_you_are.html.

Reprinted fair use and public domain. From "Get Educated: What is Domestic Violence?" by the National Domestic Violence Hotline. Researched 31 January 2013. All rights reserved. http://www.thehotline.org/get-educated/what-is-domestic-violence/.

Reprinted with permission of the publisher. From *The Secret of the Shadow: The Power of Owning Your Whole Story* ©2002 by Debbie Ford, HarperCollins Publishers, New York, NY. All rights reserved. www.harpercollins.com.

Reprinted with permission of the publisher. From *Somebodies and Nobodies: Overcoming the Abuse of Rank* ©2003 by Robert W. Fuller, New Society Publishers, Gabriola, B.C. All rights reserved. www.newsociety.com.

Reprinted with permission of the publisher. From *Attracting Perfect Customers: The Power of Strategic Synchronicity* ©2001 by Stacey Hall and Jan Brogniez, Berrett-Koehler Publishers, Inc., San Francisco, CA. All rights reserved. www.bkconnection.com.

Reprinted with permission of the publisher. From *Expect to Win: 10 Proven Strategies for Thriving in the Workplace* ©2010 by Carla A. Harris, Plume, Penguin Group, New York, NY. All rights reserved. www.us.penguingroup.com.

Reprinted with permission of the author, editor and publisher. From "Bisexuality Myths Debunked By Science," ©2012 by Samantha Joel, M.A., *Science of Relationships*, August 2, 2012. Researched 23 May 2013. All rights reserved. http://www.scienceofrelationships.com/home/2012/8/2/bisexuality-myths-debunked-by-science.html.

Reprinted fair use and public domain. From "The Symbolic Life," ©1939 by Carl Jung, a Seminar Talk for the Guild for Pastoral Psychology, London, England. Researched 30 June 2013. All rights reserved. http://www.jung.org/readingcorner.html.

Reprinted with permission of the editor Timothy Loving. From *The Science of Relationships: Answers to Your Questions About Dating, Marriage, and Family* ©2011 by Lewandowski, Gary W. Jr., PhD., Timothy J. Loving, Ph.D., Benjamin Le, Ph.D. and Marci E.J. Gleason, Ph.D., Kendall Hunt Publishing Company, Dubuque, IA. All rights reserved. www.scienceofrelationships.com.

Reprinted with permission of the author and publisher. From *Forgive for Good: A Prescription for Health and Happiness* ©2002 by Dr. Fred Luskin, Harper San Francisco, HarperCollins Publishers, New York, NY. All rights reserved. www.harpercollins.com.

Reprinted fair use and with permission of the author. From *Living Your Best Life: The Ultimate Life List Guide* ©2009 by Caroline Adams Miller, MAPP and Dr. Michael B. Frisch, Sterling Publishing, New York NY. All rights reserved. www.carolinemiller.com.

Reprinted with permission of the author and publishers. From *Self-Compassion: Stop Beating Yourself Up and Leave Insecurity Behind* ©2011 by Dr. Kristin Neff, Ph.D., William Morrow, an Imprint of HarperCollins Publishers, New York, NY. U.S., ITS Dep., Canada, Philippine islands and Open Market Territory. All rights reserved. www.harpercollins.com. Hodder and Stoughton, Hachette UK, London, England. United Kingdom and British Commonwealth. All rights reserved. http://www.hodder.co.uk.

Reprinted fair use and public domain. From "Everyday Fitness." WebMD ©2010 by Peeke, Dr. Pamela, MD, MPH, FACP. Researched 2 August 2012. All rights reserved. http://blogs.webmd.com/pamela-peeke-md/2010/01/just-what-is-an-average-womans-size-anymore.html.

Reprinted fair use and by permission of the author. From *Flourish: A Visionary New Understanding of Happiness and Well-Being* ©2011 by Dr. Martin E.P. Seligman, Free Press, New York, NY. www.authentichappiness.org.

Reprinted fair use and public domain. From *Romeo and Juliet by William Shakespeare,* 2.1.85-86.

Reprinted with permission of the publisher. From *Calling in the One: 7 Weeks to Attract the Love of Your Life* ©2004 by Katherine Woodward Thomas, Three Rivers Press, New York, NY. All rights reserved. www.randomhouse.com.

Reprinted with permission of the publisher. From *Tantra in Practice: Princeton Reading in Religions* ©2000 by David Gordon White, ed. Princeton Press, Princeton, NJ. All rights reserved. www.press.princeton.edu.

Additional Works Consulted or Referenced

Consulted fair use. http://www.binetusa.org.

Referenced fair use. From *Writing as a Way of Healing: How Telling Our Stories Transforms Our Lives* ©1999 by Louise DeSalvo, Beacon Press, Boston, MA. All rights reserved. http://www.beacon.org/.

Referenced fair use. From "Famous Bisexual People in History" by Sheela Lambert. 25 July 2013. http://www.examiner.com/article/famous-bisexuals-history.

Referenced fair use. From *The Soul Singer of Tyrnos* ©1981, 2008 by Ardath Mayhar, The Borgo Press, an Imprint of Wildside Press LLC, location. All rights reserved. http://www.wildsidepress.com.

Referenced with permission of the founder. From *The Art and Practice of Coaching (TAPOC) Training* by Julio Olalla, Newfield Network. Foundations and Ontological coach training received October 2011 to June 2012. http://www.newfieldnetwork.com.

Referenced fair use. From *The Oxford Dictionary of Current English, 3rd edition* ©2001, Oxford University Press, Oxford, England. http://global.oup.com/?cc=us.

Referenced fair use. From *Writing to Change the World* ©2006 by Mary Pipher, Riverhead Books, Penguin Group. All rights reserved. www.us.penguingroup.com.

Referenced fair use. From *The Hawaiian Dictionary, Revised and Enlarged Edition* ©1986 by Mary Kawena Pukui and Samuel H. Elbert, University of Hawaii Press, Honolulu, HI. All rights reserved. http://www.uhpress.hawaii.edu/.

Referenced fair use. From "List of International Non Profit Organizations" by Kyra Sheahan, EHow.com contributor. http://www.ehow.com/info_8000671_list-international-non-profit-organizations.html.

Referenced fair use. From *Learned Optimism: How to Change Your Mind and Your Life* ©1990 by Dr. Martin E.P. Seligman, Free Press, New York, NY. All rights reserved. www.authentichappiness.org.

Referenced fair use and public domain. From "The Empath," *Star Trek,* Season 3, Episode 12, 6 December 1968. http://www.imdb.com/title/tt0708462/.

Referenced fair use and public domain. From "Man of the People," *Star Trek: The Next Generation,* Season 6, Episode 3, 3 October 1992. http://www.imdb.com/title/tt0708746/?ref_=fn_al_tt_1.

Referenced fair use. From *Dictionary of Classical Mythology* ©1985 by J.E. Zimmerman, Bantam Books, New York, NY. All rights reserved. www.bantambooks.com.

Fair use and/or public domain epigraph quotations by:
Maya Angelou, Erma Bombeck, Joseph Campbell, Confucius, e.e. cummings, His Holiness the Dalai Lama, Sigmund Freud,

Dr. Martin Luther King, Nelson Mandela, Margaret Mead, Eleanor Roosevelt, Henry David Thoreau, Mark Twain, Lao Tzu, Marianne Williamson and Oprah Winfrey.

Epigraph quotations reprinted with permission:
Sarah Ban Breathnach, Robert W. Fuller, Debbie Ford (see above "Works Reprinted by Permission").

Foreword
by Master Coach Julio Olalla
Founder of Newfield Network

For many, many years we have dismissed the soul as a legitimate domain of learning. Our educational system has focused on studying the world as a mechanistic, materialistic process from which we are separated. From this scientific style of learning we have developed extraordinary technologies and tools of logical and linear thinking. However, the shadow side of these discoveries has led to the exploitation of our planet's riches, an increase of consumption and a separation from our own souls.

In response to abandoning our soul as a valid voice, we begin to experience a profound cry from within that demands we pay attention. It requires that we include our emotions, our spirit, our connection with nature and our relationship to each other in our definition of humanity. If we continue to dismiss human experience, the epidemic of depression and the abundance of ecological disasters will consume us. In fact many countries have had great economic growth in the last decades and at the same time experienced an insignificant growth in the happiness of their people.

Lani Kwon, MA has written a book that specifically deals with issues that I believe belong to the soul. She does not utilize a grandiose academic approach but, instead, uses storytelling to draw us into a state of reflection. Lani reveals conversations with people who went through deep transformation and includes powerful stories she herself has lived. She invites us to reflect on awareness, meaningful work and service to others, among several other topics essential to reflect and to learn from in order to create a good life. While she also shares research in the field of positive psychology, she offers insightful exercises and explorations in which we can use our own stories in order to make meaning of our own experiences.

Storytelling is an ancient and evocative way to convey powerful meaning. In place of giving us information, stories resonate with our soul and act as a catalyst for the emergence of our own great wisdom. When we are invited to dream in new ways, we access a kind of creativity that stems directly from a deep and mysterious place within us. We enter new worlds and are transported out of the confines of pure logic and into substantial meaning that feeds our soul and satiates the division we feel in modern times.

Lani brings awareness to our cultural assumptions that keep us caged in the fiction of "the way things are." Learning from someone who walks the path of personal transformation can be a great source for us when we enter a quest of expanding what is important to us and what we need in order to experience fulfillment. Read this book and allow Lani to be your storyteller. Storytelling is a ritual. It goes beyond the story itself. There is magic in stories. Let them take you on a journey to discover something new, something beautiful and something alive.

In my thirty years as a coach, I have learned that embracing the power of satisfaction, gratitude and the act of serving others are essential aspects in living a good life. You can never truly be yourself without the joy of serving others. You can never be satisfied without connecting with otherness and living with gratitude. In spite of the powerful cultural forces that predicate dissatisfaction as an economic engine, there is a deep part of your soul that knows differently. That part of you knows the essence of gratitude and the magic of living a meaningful life. We must recover the sacredness in our daily lives. We must recover our sense of connectivity with one another and nature. Read Lani's book. There you will find a sweet invitation.

Julio Olalla
Founder of Newfield Network
http://www.newfileldnetwork.com
Boulder, CO
January 28, 2013

Preface

To be nobody but yourself in a world which is doing its best, night and day, to make you everybody else means to fight the hardest battle which any human being can fight; and never stop fighting.
–e. e. cummings

Dear Reader,

    This book took a long time to write—my entire life, actually—but six years on-and-off, if you count the actual time I spent thinking about it, interviewing people, writing, organizing and editing it. During that time I became pregnant with my son, Noa, and I can't help but compare this book to a post-due baby that refused to be born in a reasonable length of time. Conception occurred when one of my clients said, "You really should write a book!" after experiencing one of the explorations I had created back in 2005.

People have told me stories about themselves throughout my entire life. Even when I was very little, I would be on the bus with my mother and sisters, and strangers would confide in me. I took this in stride. I didn't realize then that most people don't confide their deepest, darkest secrets to strangers, and especially not to young children. I did my best to listen, although I couldn't always understand. I think that people could sense that I genuinely cared, which is what drew them to me.

    I remember one time, I must have been seven or eight, when I was out and about with my family, an elderly lady was sitting at a bus stop in Makakilo, Hawai'i. She had just missed her bus and was going to be late transferring to another. Her groceries were in bags all around her. My mother suggested she call a relative or friend to come and get her or a taxi.

"Too expensive," the lady grunted, and by that I understood that she didn't have a relative or a friend to rely upon.

My mother shrugged, having done her best, and turned back to care for my sisters, who were younger than I.

I asked her, "Which would be more expensive? The taxi or losing all of your groceries?" I didn't say this in a judgmental way. I could see she had some frozen items in the bags, and even though they were frozen now, they wouldn't last for long in Hawai'i's heat and humidity.

She nodded and then trudged away towards the strip mall across the street. It felt good being helpful to someone else who needed support and being able to clarify the situation in such a way whereby she could then make her own decision.

In a sense I have always been a life coach. When I was that same age, seven or eight, my mother confided things in me that she probably shouldn't have: concerns about my father, their marriage and their financial troubles. I was and still am the friend that friends come to for advice. I was also the designated driver, key holder and third wheel on several dates in high school and college, which wasn't as much fun. In short, people tell me stuff. I learned very early on how to keep a secret. These are qualities that come in handy in this line of work: caring, problem-solving, confidentiality.

This is a book of stories. Some people may disparage self-help books that include personal stories, but I find them to be vital in the work that I do. I have found that other people's stories are affirming, uplifting and healing. Several former clients, mentors and body-mind-spirit practitioners have shared their stories with me in interviews, and I am grateful to them for being willing to share their sometimes traumatic but always transcendent stories with you. Storytelling is one of the earliest ways that human beings communicated important values, morals and social norms to one another. Stories are still important today.

You may find at times that some of the stories and exercises are deeply moving or even disturbing. You may also be triggered by past traumas of your own of which you may or may not have been aware. Please take good care of yourself. Do not force it. Forcing change is like prying open the petals of a bud before it is ready to bloom into a flower. Treat yourself like you would your best friend. Reach out for support, if you need it: counselors, therapists, coaches, mentors, clergy, family and friends who love you and are non-judgmental are the best refuge.

I also include hands-on explorations and practices at the end of each chapter. I recommend approaching these in a mood of curiosity. I divide them into "If you have 5 to 10 minutes…" and "If you have more time…" sections. Remember: You are not being graded on these, and no one needs to see your entries, unless you want them to. This book is for your benefit and delight. You should do only those explorations that you can devote your attention, care and time to. The more you do the deeper you'll go, but it's okay to skip sections and come back to them later.

Finally, I was inspired by the over thirty-plus years of scientific positive psychology research on the topics of optimism, vulnerability, goal-setting, determination and self-compassion. Researchers, coaches and writers such as Dr. Martin E.P. Seligman, Dr. Kristin Neff, Katherine Woodward Thomas, M.A., M.F.T., Caroline Adams Miller M.A.P.P., Brené Brown, LMSW, Ph.D. and Amy Cuddy, Ph.D. stand out in particular. I have quoted many of them in this book, because their research is cutting edge, thought-provoking and has relevant applications. You can use their discoveries to make your own life better.

In *The Creating CoPOWERment® Workbook* you will:

- Discover what motivates you and utilize strengths to create your ideal life.
- Learn how your unexamined thoughts and beliefs hold you back from achieving your goals.
- Transform these obstacles into lessons and markers of success.
- Align with like-minded-hearted-souled allies, organizations and communities.
- Find out what your life purpose really is and step-by-step how to get there.

I hope that you find this book to be eye-opening and enlightening and that it will support you in transforming your life for the better.

Me ke aloha (with love),
Lani Kwon, MA
Founder of the Creating CoPOWERment® Center LLC
August 12, 2013

Know Thyself

Awareness and Inner Peace

*He who knows others is wise.
He who knows himself is enlightened.*
–Lao Tzu

Monkey Mind

In this day and age, it's difficult to find places of peace. We're surrounded by constant noise. Have you noticed that, even walking along the sidewalk, we're often bombarded by advertising or music deliberately broadcasting on loudspeakers? Commercials now run in what used to be public space. People shout into their cell phones, and there's no way to avoid unintentionally overhearing conversations. Our attention is diverted by multiple sensations. We may sometimes feel overwhelmed by the hustle and bustle of modern life. However, it is possible, even in this boisterous chaos, to create moments of awareness and clarity, to create inner peace.

It begins with awareness.

When we are unconscious of our thoughts, feelings and, thus, our motivations, we are at the mercy of physical sensations, emotional impulses and unmindful reactivity. We cannot be present, much less still. We bounce from one thought, feeling or reaction to another. "Monkey mind" is what the Buddhists call this incessant hyperactivity. In this unrestful state of suffering, we misperceive our true selves and our place in the world. We misperceive others. It is only when we become the aware observer of all of our experiences—not the fluctuating feelings, thoughts or sensations—that we can be free. This discovery process requires moments of silence.

On the Value of Silence

Even a few minutes of silence per day can encourage a person to pay attention to his or her internal world. Each of us can carve out this time in such mundane moments as sitting at a stoplight or even while standing in line:

1) Turn off the radio and cell phone.
2) Take a deep breath and simply notice.
3) At the office, if possible, close the door and unplug the phone during breaks, just for a few minutes.
4) Stop multi-tasking. Focus on one thing at a time.
5) Go outside at lunchtime, walk or drive to a park or another peaceful location nearby.

Notice how these simple steps impact the rest of your day. In each moment we have an opportunity to make informed choices, rather than react out of habit. We can recognize our habitual ways of reacting, and then in the pause created by our awareness, we will have clarity about the right actions to take in the right time and in the right place.

On Meditation

Recently, I have noticed that much of my suffering is caused by inappropriate reactions to events, people or things around me. When I am aware of this, I am much more capable of mindful choices, rather than knee-jerk reactions. The ability to discern what is really happening, how people are really behaving or what something actually is allows me an opportunity to choose the right course of action, if any is required. I've discovered that simply noticing events, people and objects is enough. Sometimes I can just let things be as they are, instead of taking inappropriate action.

When I discovered meditation in my late twenties, it was a blessing. However, it was not easy at first. Even with the support of experienced teachers, meditation brought up painful feelings and thoughts I had repressed for many years. As a child I was molested and sexually assaulted by acquaintances of my parents. It was enough to terrify me, and it led to deeply ingrained feelings of shame in my adolescence and early adulthood. When I started meditating, I needed additional support to handle the painful reality I had long ago sought to bury. I was fortunate to have a partner, friends and counselors who helped me sort through the past, confirm that the present was worth living and that I could create a better future.

If meditation scares you, there may very well be a reason. If you find that you uncover frightened parts of yourself that have been dormant for a long time, I recommend you reach out for support from a trusted friend, family member, spouse, minister and/or counselor. Post-traumatic stress disorder can impact people years after a traumatic event has occurred. It is incredibly empowering to uncover your past and own it, all of it, even the painful parts of your life.

In *Flourish: A Visionary New Understanding of Happiness and Well-Being*, Dr. Martin E.P. Seligman puts forward the groundbreaking idea of post-traumatic growth, writing:

> A few years ago, Chris Peterson, Nansook Park, and I added a link to my Authentic Happiness website www.authentichappiness.org. The new questionnaire listed fifteen worst things that can happen in a person's life: torture, grave illness, death of a child, rape, imprisonment, and so on. In a month, 1,700 people reported at least one of these awful events, and they took our well-being tests as well. To our surprise, individuals who'd experienced one awful event had

more intense strengths (and therefore higher well-being) than individuals who had none. Individuals who had been through two awful events were stronger than individuals who had one, and individuals who had three—raped, tortured and held captive for example—were stronger than those who had two.[1]

Our traumas can actually enhance our strengths and lead us forward to better lives. We can harness awareness, ask for help and receive the support needed to make meaning of difficult experiences in our lives. It is important to understand that we did the best we could, considering the situation in the past, and also that we do not have to remain stuck in the past or hurt in the present. It is possible to take everything we encounter, even tragic and traumatic events, and to create a brighter and better future, using our strengths, resources and resilience.

Vipassana and Metta Meditation

There are many forms of meditation. Western variations include the silent reflection found in the Christian faith. The practice I have personally found to be helpful for awareness is the Buddhist practice called *vipassana*, or mindfulness meditation. In *vipassana* I notice myself breathing in and out. I notice how the breath feels on my lip or in my nostrils. Sometimes I count, "One. Two. Three. Four…," the in-breath and out-breath and the pauses that occur before breathing in and breathing out. I become aware of my thoughts, physical sensations, feelings and anything else that is happening around me. I notice my reactions to external events, sounds and stimuli. I come back to my breath. I come back to the present moment, and I become aware of the observer Self who has awakened. I become awake to the other parts of myself that are habitually in control.

Another useful practice I have found is *metta*, or loving-kindness meditation. There are many variations of *metta*, but at the heart of all of them is the active practice of wishing yourself, those you love, those you like, those you feel neutral towards, those you dislike and those you may think you hate the same levels of peace, happiness and freedom from suffering. I expand my capacity for love and equanimity by practicing this meditation. I become aware that we all suffer and that we all want to be free from suffering. *Vipassana* allows for an opening of the consciousness, while *metta* allows for an opening of the heart. Both allow for awareness, clarity and realization of the Self.

Ironically, when I least have the time or inclination to meditate, I most need to do it. For example, as I write and edit this book, I have been struggling with some past memories that came up during meditation. I am upset by my current thoughts and feelings about them. Yet sifting through these recollections and reactions as they surface, allowing myself to feel and think and then to breathe through them, I found gold among the dirt and stones. I have been able to pick out these nuggets and polish them and share them in this book for what I hope is the benefit of others struggling with similar traumas in their lives.

In awareness we have choice, and with choice we have the potential for inner peace.

An Interview with a Practitioner of Body-Mind-Spirit Awareness
Master Wasentha Young of Peaceful Dragon School

www.peacefuldragonschool.com
wasentha@peacefuldragonschool.com

I was fortunate to know many adept practitioners, counselors and healers when I lived in Ann Arbor, Michigan. I am also grateful to call Master Wasentha Young, who is the owner and director of the Peaceful Dragon School of T'ai Chi Ch'uan and Chi Kung, a friend. In addition to training in T'ai Chi since 1968, she has a background in Taoist and Buddhist meditation, has earned certificates in Acupressure and as a Wellness Counselor in Mind-Body Consciousness, and holds a Master's degree in Transpersonal Studies from the Institute of Transpersonal Psychology in California. Wasentha is an African-American woman with a ready smile and a youthful beauty that belies her experience and wisdom. She is forthright in a way that some might find intimidating, but those who truly know her admire her and appreciate her wit. She is fascinated by the interconnections between body, mind and spirit. She is well versed in the study and practice of awareness.

When I interviewed her, we sat in my living room on a wintry evening in 2009, each with a hot mug of tea clasped in our hands to warm them. I began by asking what first interested her about becoming more aware.

She replied, "Someone once asked me, 'Can you imagine who we'd be if we used more of our brains?' It motivated me to open up my conscious awareness and become more present to the influences of the unconscious." In essence Wasentha was suggesting that awareness is an ongoing process and not an end result.

She explained, "In being present to the unconscious, I can feel a vibration of something like a distant drum, buzz or light. For me this awareness is being conscious of being unconscious, feeling the connection of everyday reality and the fabric of dream/unconscious costuming my awake state."

This was a lot of information to take in at first, and I could see she had given the topic of awareness a great deal of thought and consideration over the years. Wasentha was touching upon more than just being aware of thoughts, feelings, sensations and/or events or situations as they were in each moment. She was talking about delving deeper into the subconscious thoughts, unconscious motivations and reflex actions that create "reality," like the man behind the curtain in *The Wizard of Oz*. She was talking about awareness of awareness.

Wasentha continued, "There is a tangible relationship you can connect between the conscious and the unconscious through awareness. In T'ai Chi and Chi Kung, which translates as 'energy work,' it starts as the physical body informing the mind; at a certain point in study, the mind informs the body, to developing the awareness of the continuous dialogue between mind, body and spirit. At this point the practice becomes sensual: physical, mental and spiritual."

I asked, "So the physical practice of T'ai Chi and Chi Kung are actually entryways to mental and spiritual awareness?" I was still trying to expand my consciousness and take in everything she was saying. She nodded, but as she did, I realized it was more than that. She was saying that there was an interrelationship between the physical, mental and spiritual and that each of these seemingly separate categories were interconnected.

"Many people call them physical forms of meditation that can be practiced regularly to achieve awareness. What advice do you have for those wanting to become more aware?" I asked, expecting her to advise practicing T'ai Chi or Chi Kung, but her response surprised me.

"I absolutely advocate nature as a vehicle to help with awareness."

"Nature?"

"Yes, I have an exercise I share with students. I find a path at the edge of a woodsy or natural environment in nature. I bow to the path and say to myself, 'Nature becomes my consciousness.' From that point every step I take is an adventure into myself. What I see, hear, smell and even taste on the path becomes a reflection of my consciousness."

"The outward reflects the inward?" I asked, rhetorically, in order to help myself understand where she was going with this idea. "And vice versa?"

Wasentha elaborated, "Nature doesn't have a prescribed pattern. It can be reflective of different aspects of our consciousness. You can explore so many aspects of your states of being in this way. You can access awareness through the body, mind, and spirit as parts of the whole."

Her description of this process made me want to try it at a local park.

"I personally prefer embodied styles of meditations, but you can still reach awareness without having a particular practice," she said.

It was liberating to hear that there were many paths to becoming more aware and that different methods work for different people. Yet, this was the first time I had heard from anyone that people didn't need a particular practice in order to become more aware.

She continued, "There are so many styles of meditation."

I pondered this new angle in understanding awareness, and I took a deep breath and was aware of it.

"A lot of times, it has to do with perspectives." Wasentha said, "I tell my students the main components to awareness are: 'We relax down. We open up. We reflect. We change.'

Awareness is not centered in the mind, body or spirit but rather in open relationships."

Wasentha concluded, getting up from her chair, "You will feel more vulnerable as you become more aware. Ironically, it is when we start becoming aware that we feel more." She paused and smiled slightly. "Know that there is strength in vulnerability and be aware of your filters. Trust in the intelligence of your awareness."

It was the first time someone had ever suggested that being more vulnerable was a sign of awakening and that vulnerability could be a strength. I thanked my friend, Wasentha, for this insight. She was saying that awareness meant feeling more. It was transcendent conversation for which I am grateful to share.

Inner Peace Explorations:

If you have 5 to 10 minutes, answer the following:

Do you allow yourself moments of silence and space to create it? How often?

What other ways do you cultivate awareness and clarity in your life? (e.g. martial arts, art, sports, prayer, etc…)

Have there been moments when you've noticed your habitual reactions to people, events or things? How did you react? Are you able to go with the flow or pause before taking action?

Who in your life can support you in creating opportunities for more silence, awareness and clarity?

Is there anything that comes into your consciousness during meditation that is in need of healing? If so, what is it? What resources, people and practices can you cultivate to experience post-traumatic growth?

If you have more time:

Look into a form of meditation that interests you. You can try *vipassana*, *metta* or another technique. Or, if you prefer physical movement to stillness, try walking in nature, as Master Young suggested. Or, perhaps, you could try yoga or T'ai Chi or another martial art? You may wish to sign up for a class or buy or rent a CD or DVD for initial guidance in one of these forms. Or you can go into nature with the intention of being present and aware. I encourage you to stick with your chosen practice, form or activity for at least a full month. It may be uncomfortable or frustrating at first, but as you deepen your practice, you will begin to observe increased awareness and find precious insights. Write these down in a journal or record them. Polish these insights and allow your budding awareness to light your way.

Names Have Meanings.
Words Have Power.

What's in a name? That which we call a rose by any other word would smell as sweet.
–William Shakespeare's Romeo and Juliet 2.1.85-86

What Meaning is in a Name?

What really is in a name? Is it really true that if someone were named Ichabod it would still sound as sweet as Nathaniel? How about what each one means? "Glory is gone" and "God has given," respectively. Most people in this day and age are unaware of what their names mean. Some may check a baby name book or online when selecting a name for their child but only glance at the meaning of their own names, if at all.

Celebrities often change their names, or their agents and publicists do it for them, to catchy, attention-getting names, although it's debatable if John Cougar was actually better than John Mellancamp. Not to mention the bizarre names some of them give to their children. Our nicknames also define us and sometimes describe us better than our given names, but Babs and Jimbo are preferable to Stinky. The prefixes and suffixes in a name also define who we are: Ms. versus Miss or Mrs., Mr. or Dr., Sir and Jr. and the highfalutin III. Names have meanings. Words have power. That which we think and say, becomes what we do and who we become.

Many Native American cultures gave private spirit names, as well as offering public nicknames, careful to guard the essence of who they were from enemies, and only sharing their private names with close friends and family. I have also read that Native Americans believe that they should not call a baby by their given name because then the child might be called back to the spirit world.

In Hawaiian culture babies often were not gifted with their full names until their first birthday. Part of the reason for this was that in the past it was uncertain if a child would reach his or her first birthday. But the deeper, spiritual reason is that the family, the grandparents in particular, wanted to know and understand who the child was before bestowing a name upon them. Even today, often only the elders in the 'ohana (family) know the child's full name. They do not make it public until the child grows into his or her name, taking into consideration the child's personality, while honoring the parents and the child's familial lineage and cultural heritage with a Hawaiian name.

Unfortunately, both of my grandparents on Maui had passed away when my son was born, and so I chose the name "Noa" because it means "freedom from kapu" (restrictions), though there have been moments in his toddlerhood when I have wished I'd named him something that meant "careful" or "patience" instead.

Names, like all words, have the power to manifest one's destiny.

How Names Have the Power to Manifest Your Destiny

A dear friend of mine, Janis, was first named "Jane" by her father, but another woman in the hospital's delivery room had just named her daughter Jane, and Janis' mother did not wish her to think they were copying her. Janis is a professional massage therapist, Rolfist, occupational therapist and mother to a grown daughter. She meditates on a daily basis and is a practicing Tibetan Buddhist. There is nothing plain-Jane about Janis anyway, and her mother's last-minute correction accurately reflects her spirit. Janis told me that the Greco-Roman god, Janus, has three heads, one looking forward into the future, one looking back into the past and one that looks within. According to *The Dictionary of Classical Mythology*, Janus was "the god of beginnings, openings, entrances, doorways and endings."[2] This name couldn't be more true about her.

A client and, later, good friend of mine was given the name of her mother's adoptive mother, Louise, which means "renowned fighter." It is the feminine form of Louis. Even though it is a courageous name, she never felt comfortable with it. It chafed and contained her free spirit. To her it was an older woman's name, a name popular in another era, a name that invoked someone once loved who was now dead. When Louise went through a major life change in her early thirties, switching from a career on Wall Street to studying and teaching yoga, healing modalities and meditation, she experienced a metamorphosis. It took over a year, but she received the inspiration during meditation to change her name to Sura, a Sanskrit word meaning "God." It was a name she says, "Felt more me," and one "I felt comfortable with, and even delighted to hear when someone called me, 'Sura.'" Her traditional, Korean-American father had a difficult time understanding why Sura chose to do this, but her mother, who is more intuitive, understood completely. Louise was their child, and Sura is a child of the Universe. She needed a new name in order to bring to life her Divine Purpose. "Sura" more accurately reflects who she is and will become.

I first met Dan at a holiday party in 2012. I was struck by his ephemeral beauty and grace. He looked like an elf in *The Lord of the Rings* or an angel. His voice had a lilting quality that was pleasant to the ears, his hair was golden and his skin fair, and his energy was soothing and energizing at the same time. Dan was born in California, raised in Houston, Texas, and he was studying drama, Chinese opera and fine art in Honolulu. His name story began when his father expected his first-born son to be named "Butch." He told me, "My mother and both grandmothers weren't happy about it. They were worried I would be rebellious like my father but went along with it, even though they always called me Danny." He had a happy childhood, unaware of the implications of a name like "Butch," until high school, when he already knew that he was different. "I tried to be invisible, kept as quiet as I could. I was living with my grandmother at the time, and she preferred quiet. In high school I was able to get by relatively unnoticed." After he graduated with a GED, he chose to go by the name Daniel, his middle name, instead of his given first name in college. Dan later performed in elaborate and elegant drag as Nini Delorean, Nini Majestique, Madama Nightingale, Madama Nightingale Iróke (which is a Japanese term used by *geisha*, meaning covert sex appeal and seemingly unintentional, though purposeful, glamour) and, finally, Pearl Dynasty. These name choices were significant. Names not only identify our gender, our sex and sexuality, our culture of origin and family, they also describe our spirit and sense of self. For a young man who is also an embodied woman, the need to find an appropriate set of names is more than just vanity or fashion trend. It is a way to identify his/her true self, to create a persona and personhood that most of the world may not fully understand. As Dan/Pearl put it so eloquently, "One of the reasons I became the opposite of the name I was given was to even out the intentions behind it. Sometimes I just want to dress like a woman, and other times I like to dress as a man. I wanted my drag character to be a source of light. It was about finding my own voice." Dan/Pearl has decided to live his/her life differently, authentically. Recently s/he reclaimed his/her given name, "Butch," by including it in his/her e-mail address and school application forms. I have also given my friend the nicknames Daring Darling Dan and Passionflower Pearl. Our nicknames, those names given to us by friends out of affection, create new opportunities for self-expression. The names and identities we choose for ourselves are even more relevant.

My name, Lani Kwon, also truly represents who I am. "Lani," according to *The Hawaiian Dictionary* by Mary Kawena Pukui and Samuel H. Elbert, means "sky, heaven; heavenly, spiritual."[3] However, I didn't like my name as a child. There were no mugs or key chains sold in gift stores that bore my name. No T-shirts with the name "Lani" transferred onto their fronts. And, most irritating of all, there was a mascot for a local dairy where I had gone on a field trip with my fifth grade class, a stupid cow named "Lani Moo." Imagine a class of fifth graders with that taunt.

I complained to my parents one day, "Why didn't you name me Lynn or Liz…or something normal?" I wanted an English name, an American name, not some weird Hawaiian name I couldn't fully appreciate at that time.

My mother grew up in Pennsylvania and, later, in Southern California, where she had met and married my father, who was born and raised on Maui. In 1969 they were stationed in Brunswick, Georgia. My dad was in the Navy at the time, heading off to war in Vietnam, when I was conceived and born in America's Deep South. The name "Lani" must have given him comfort. "Your father wanted to remember that he was from Hawai'i," mom replied.

My sister Lea pointed out that many of the street names in Hawai'i are variations of "Lani": Kapi'olani, Lili'oukalani, Ka'iulani. "There's no Kapi'olea Boulevard!" she protested, and we giggled. My sister, Laura, added, "Or any Lili'oukalaura Avenue." It was then that I started to appreciate my name.

Often people ask me if it's just "Lani," not "Leilani" or

"Kailani" or some other variation? I affirm, "Yes, just Lani." I know I am Lani and that my familial name, "Kwon," means "authority" or "power" in Korean. My married name for nineteen years was "Meilgaard," which means "Meil's Farm" in Danish. Thus, I feel that the full meaning of my name translates into "heavenly power" brought down to Earth.

Names Have Meanings, Words Have Power Explorations:

If you have 5 to 10 minutes, answer the following:

Look up in a baby name book or online the meaning(s) of your first, middle and last names. Write them down.

Do these names match who you know yourself to be? Who you are becoming?

Are there any other names you've come across that appeal to you?

Were there nicknames, pet names or made-up names in your childhood that held special meaning for you? Who gave you those names? Did they match who you were? Do they still signify who you are and who you are becoming?

If you have more time, answer the following:

Do you wish to keep your given names, or would you rather take on a new name(s)?

If so, what is your real name, the name that manifests who you really are?

If you are planning to have a child or children, what qualities would you like your child/ren to have? Which names embody these qualities?

Ego Boost

You have to actually have an ego before you can give it up.
—Marianne Williamson

Defining the Ego

What is "ego"? *The Oxford Dictionary of Current English, 3rd edition*, defines "ego" as "1) a person's self-esteem; 2) Psychoanalysis: the part of the mind that is responsible for the interpretation of reality and the sense of self."[4] In fact the father of psychoanalysis, Sigmund Freud, considered the ego to be the organized and conscious balance between the unruly, unconscious id and the authoritarian, parental superego. For many of my coaching clients going through transition, it is a challenging experience to separate the idea of ego as being selfish or overly self-absorbed from the concept of a healthy self-esteem and self worth. I have seen many people who are embarrassed, concerned or even ashamed to be "acting out of ego." Yet, without a positive sense of self, we are easy targets for unscrupulous gurus, con artists and corrupt leaders. "Start from where you are," I tell them. "You don't need to be Gandhi or the Buddha or Mother Teresa. You simply need to be yourself, to figure out who you are and who you want to be, and to do your best to continue to do your best." You can pay attention to what gives you joy and what causes you sorrow, noticing how you react and interact with others and choosing in each moment how you want to behave.

In recent years the word "ego" has become a dirty word. Many New Age authors and spiritual teachers and their books,

CDs, DVDs, websites and other modes of (somewhat ironic) self-expression damn the ego. They call for an end to the ego or, at the very least, counsel a reduction of it, leading to an awakening to a belief in unity or oneness. While there is nothing wrong in believing and working toward unity and a sense of interconnectedness, I have noticed how people use this philosophy to beat up themselves or others. People who are constantly self-sacrificing or over-giving are not doing anyone a favor, while those who require or expect others to be egoless may have ulterior motives. Egotism is mindless and always puts the self first at the expense of others, while a healthy ego is mindful with the ability to think, speak and act with the highest good of all concerned in mind, heart and spirit. A healthy sense of self, while acknowledging our interconnectedness, allows for compassion for oneself and others.

Creating CoPOWERment®

When I first began designing Creating CoPOWERment® workshops in 2003, I knew I was here to serve and support others going through transition. I had been through many life transitions myself, including graduation, recovery from a chronic injury and depression, career changes and relationship challenges, but I wasn't entirely sure how or what the best way to serve would be. I worked as a crisis counselor for non-profit organizations, taught English and writing, was a volunteer coordinator and worked at retail stores. Through all of these experiences I recognized that "Service" to me meant listening and hearing what each person was saying, asking questions when I didn't understand and being kind to each person I came in contact with to the best of my ability. It also meant learning to be kind to myself.

The need for a healthy ego became clear when I was

working as a crisis counselor at a domestic violence shelter and rape crisis hotline in 2004. Many people in this setting did not take good care of themselves. It was unvoiced, but there was the strong expectation that everyone should make additional personal sacrifices above and beyond the call of duty, as if that would somehow illustrate how devoted we were to our clients. A couple of my co-workers on the crisis line would not take a lunch break. It put pressure on me to be able to work without a break. In the end I got a note from my doctor explaining that, due to fainting spells, I could not be expected to work an eight-hour shift without a break. It took ego, in the positive sense of that word, to learn to care for my own well-being and assert the right to self.

I have to start from where I am, which means from moment to moment, noticing what is going on around me and inside me. I have feelings, thoughts and moods, and sometimes these are in conflict with one another. I think of this as occurring on a sliding continuum. We can become aware of our habitual actions, thoughts and choices. However, there will be moments of forgetting, "spiritual amnesia." There will be times when we are overwhelmed and overreact or numb out and are too tired to care. To treat oneself poorly because we have not yet attained "enlightenment" is as silly as expecting a child to grow up in an instant. We are human, and we need to honor wherever we are first and to start from there. Yet if we pay attention and start from where we are, we honor who we are and who we are capable of becoming.

An Interview with Sifu Greg Knollmeyer
T'ai Chi instructor Spiral Chi Center
and Peaceful Dragon School

www.http://spiralchicenter.com

Sifu Greg Knollmeyer is a gifted T'ai Chi teacher at Spiral Chi Center and Peaceful Dragon School in Ypsilanti and Ann Arbor, Michigan, as well as a compassionate energy healer, who has studied the techniques of Reflexolo-chi and Psych-K, utilizing these in his thriving practice. He is very tall, yet moves with the grace, strength and centeredness I've seen in yogis, dancers and martial arts practitioners, people who are aware of and awake in their bodies. I interviewed him in 2009 and was so moved by his responses to my questions that I wanted to include his insight in full in this chapter on embracing the parts of ourselves that many times we push away.

Lani: What advice would you offer to those going through transition?

Greg: I think it differs from person to person. My advice is to try to recognize, as often as possible, what your actual, authentic needs are, and then adapt the meeting of those needs to whatever the situation is. And I think that often, at least in my case, I've made sacrifices that I didn't consider, that just happened. The empty room was where I would practice T'ai Chi and yoga. It was where I would sit and meditate, and there wasn't anything in there, but I didn't pack up my space and take it with me. Ultimately, it was like a pianist giving away his piano, and wanting to play at the local hotel or the local café or the local college, but not having his piano at home. It's not like I stopped being able to play or that I stopped playing. I was practicing T'ai Chi, but I didn't have that one space. The sacrifice had happened before I was aware of it, and that was jarring.

In the end I might have done the same thing or might have arranged with a friend to set up a private space, but I wasn't able in that moment to recognize what my authentic need was and somehow adapt. There's the balance of one's needs with the needs of others around us—your family or community—but it's not hedonistic to find what is an authentic need, when you're going through transition.

Lani: Yes, it's about being aware of and honest about what our needs are.

Greg: I think I sometimes also make the mistake of thinking I'm much more enlightened than I am. (He chuckled, self-deprecating, at this point.) So I'll think I can practice in public, at the park or at the Y, and that I'll be just as grounded as if I had a private space. The reality is I can do a bit of that, but I'm not so enlightened as not to know when someone is watching.

Eventually, I will cultivate a space in our next house, but we don't always need a complete fix. For now, I have found ways to practice in private occasionally. It's the recognition of the authentic need that counts, and much greater than that is allowing for a deeper appreciation of the realization and allowing for a continual evolution toward harmony.

Lani: Of our needs and the needs of others?

Greg: Yes, it's not the denial of "I may not get what I want," it's the freedom of the realization of the thoughts, actions, feelings and beliefs that matters, allowing for a greater depth of realization.

Lani: It's the recognition, not just the outcome, that is the gift, or the realization that we have a stuck belief that things should be a certain way?

Greg: Yes, that has been probably what has helped me more than anything else. That what's going on and my reactions to it are pointing to something subconsciously stuck, something more going on. Can I get to the cause of the cause, to the subconscious belief or rationalization? What is the opportunity? What can we learn?

Lani: It sounds like what you would recommend to those going through transition is to go within?

Greg: Yes, but you can also do this with assistance. You can seek out a therapist, a practitioner, et cetera, but you also bring a certain willingness. There's got to be some willingness and some personal contemplation of it. But I don't want to say that it's all willingness. You can have willingness and the wrong technique or the wrong point of entry.

A bee can die flying into the window, or it can fly away from the window and out the door, but if it doesn't know that it's flying into a window because it can't see the glass, it's not a lack of willingness of wanting to get out. But if I'm the bee going up against that window, after a while I'm getting tired and nothing's moving, then I know I need to look somewhere else. And I may need someone else's help as I'm looking. It's always about moving something subconsciously and energetically. Because the stuff that's easy to talk about is talked about.

Lani: Exactly, it's the stuff we're not aware of or that's painful to be aware of. What do you do with clients who are stuck in this way? What are some of the things you do to encourage them to go deeper, if they're ready to go deeper?

Greg: There are a number of things. I often just gently introduce a little bit of truth.

Lani: Meeting them where they're at?

Greg: Where they're at. So, for example there was a woman who was experiencing an awful lot of foot pain. I was working with her, and she said she had plantar fasciitis and suffers from fibromyalgia. Now, I'm working with her, and she's experiencing changes. I mentioned that there may be a correlation between her physical pain and something emotional that she experienced in the past. Science shows a correlation between asthma and depression, depression and smoking.

So I asked her, "Is there anything that you experienced that you can think of that is related to the pain in your feet?" She said, "Oh, that's interesting. My ex-husband broke my foot, accidentally, by shutting it in a car door. I always associate that with my ex-husband." So she wasn't ready just yet to fully integrate that past emotional experience with her current physical pain, but it introduced just a little bit more truth into the equation.

When I work with people in terms of energy work, we talk a lot about "melding." And "melding" is when I'm trying to meet you exactly where you are. It is the perfect handshake. I liken it to working *with* you rather than working on you. When we work with the person from where they are at, we work more quickly and, more importantly, we move in a way that's much more integrated.

Lani: So there's a respect there for the client? Not everyone is ready. We're at different places in our lives.

Greg: Yes, there should be no force involved. I can provide the information, and it's gentle, integrated, melded and compelling. But if they say, "No," all I can do is be willing and accept that. If there's an opportunity that comes up again, then I might make that offer again, when they're ready to hear. It's a recognition of the fact that they're healing, that there are releases in the mind and releases in the body. They are healing. It is they who grow the new cells, release energy blockages or embrace new beliefs. It's their path, their body, their healing.

Lani: Is there anything else you'd like to add that we haven't yet covered?

Greg: I think I've gone on for quite a bit (laughing). Basically, it is a repeated exercise of trying to get to what is authentic. So, I can say, "This is happening. How am I creating or contributing to this? In what ways can I adapt?" It's a repeated exercise. That's what allows us to successfully adapt.

Lani: Thank you so much for your time and insight.

The Need for a Healthy "Ego"

We must first be aware of and accept all parts of ourselves, including our egos. The ego, as annoying as it can sometimes be with all its worries, paranoia and neuroses, is there to protect our sense of selfhood. It serves a purpose and, as long as it is not the only one completely in control, it does its job well. Yet it is up to our "observer" selves, the calm, more objective part of who we are, the one who can witness the ego, to decide how to use all of our abilities. "Ego," in the healthy sense of that word, is about awareness and acceptance of ourselves, so that we will act from the better parts of ourselves.

I believe that there is a Divine reason for all of our experiences as human beings, including having an ego. With some helpful insight and support from a counselor or minister or coach or friends and family, we can choose more wisely and skillfully. At the heart of all healing is self-acceptance. We are here to be Divine human expressions of Spirit, egos and all.

Ego Boost Explorations:

If you have 5 to 10 minutes, answer the following:

What does the word "ego" mean to you?

What memories and associations do you have with the word "ego"?

Who shaped your perceptions of what an ego is and what it does?

What personality traits or qualities are important to you? Why?

If you have more time, answer the following:

What are some ways that you can accept and love all of yourself and others, even the parts you label negatively?

How can you change your own behavior(s) to be more in alignment with the traits and qualities you value?

Who Do You Think You Are?

Nobody can make you feel inferior without your consent.
—Eleanor Roosevelt

Be Yourself?

"Just be yourself" is the advice we often give children and teenagers when they are faced with peer pressure and difficult choices. What we adults forget is that it took time, experience and growth for us to discover exactly who the "Self" is, if we ever do fully discover it. When discovering, uncovering and recovering the Self, we need time. We also need courage and support. So to say, "Just be yourself" to a child or young adult is like saying, "Don't worry; you'll be fine" to someone who is grieving and in pain. These are reflex words meant to comfort the speaker more than the listener. Like children faced with challenging circumstances, we need understanding, compassion and unconditional love.

I was twelve, in that awkward time after the onset of puberty, and I had no idea who I was. Both of my sisters drew, painted and did art projects at home for fun. My mother was an artist and craftswoman, selling her miniatures and doll creations at my parents' gift store and local art fairs. My paternal grandmother dabbled in oil painting and taught dance and poetry. My father, grandfather and all of his siblings were musicians. Although I wrote stories and poetry from the age of nine, I wanted to find another mode of expressing myself. I wanted something more visual and kinetic, and something outside of my angst-ridden teenage thoughts. So I signed up for an elective art class in the seventh grade. On a side note, I should tell you that this was the same year I made the mistake of trying to cut my own bangs right before yearbook pictures were to be taken. My foray into the world of the visual arts was not unlike this unfortunate incident.

I was excited, and with my savings I bought the items on the class list of supplies at an art store downtown the week before class began. I had sharpened all my color pencils, fingered the charcoal and oil pastels. I bought a tray of "adult" watercolors, which were twice as expensive and of better quality than the usual kiddie paints you could get at the drugstore. I loved the way these materials smelled, sort of metallic and unfamiliar, yet full of promise. I also bought a drawing pad that covered my torso and thighs like a human billboard when I carried it, as well as a gray gummy eraser that squished when you pinched it and smelled like rubber. I was ready.

The first week of class, several kids sauntered in late. Each time the teacher, who shall remain unnamed, gave them what we call in Hawaiian Pidgin English "stink eye." We were coming in to class after lunch and recess, so it wasn't uncommon to have a few stragglers, but she was rigid about timing, expecting us to be there at the top of the hour and to leave exactly when the bell rang. This teacher was in her mid-thirties, and she had a strident voice, pale face and wild black hairs that stood out straight from her head in all directions.

We started with the basics: lines and shading, primary colors and secondary colors, the color wheel. Some assignments were straightforward, "Draw a portrait of a classmate." Some were more abstract and complex, "Draw anger" or "Draw love." Some were assigned as homework, and some we needed to complete during class time.

One day our teacher asked us to draw our shoes, using charcoal pencils, and told us that we had only the class time in which to complete the assignment. I was wearing an old pair of sneakers and was disappointed I wasn't wearing pumps or sandals that would be easier and nicer to draw. As I started the assignment, I took my shoes off and was self-conscious about being in my stinky socks—as it was hot and humid that afternoon—and especially because I was sitting next to a boy I liked. I was hesitant about how to draw my Reeboks, but I started with the rubber base. It gave me a platform to start from and was relatively simple, just a long curve and straight lines. Then I drew in the upper part, made of synthetic material and canvas. I was surprised by how intricate the stitching was and how beautiful the shoelaces, grommets and patterning were. I had never noticed this before. Instead of worrying about how the final product would look in comparison to my classmates', I found myself caught up in the flow, time stood still, and I was actually enjoying the process of drawing.

"You were supposed to draw both shoes," the teacher said from behind me, startling me out of my trance. When I turned to look at her, she was not smiling. She sighed heavily and then snatched my drawing from my hands before I could finish it. "Time's up."

I was crushed.

I had devoted so much time to drawing one shoe, that I had not realized there would not be time for the other. I had enjoyed what I was doing and cared about finishing it, but the teacher didn't. She was trying to keep us on schedule, within the curriculum, a structure that ironically didn't really allow for creative flow or artistic expression.

"Just be yourself," my mother had tried to comfort me after school.

"What does that even mean?" I cried, running to my room and slamming the door. I hurled my backpack on the bed, and it bounced off and fell with a thud to the floor. I lay down on my bed and stared at the ceiling.

Who am I? Who do you think you are? I thought, then felt, *No artist…my sisters are artists…but at least I'm a writer.* It was the first time I had thought of myself that way. It was a limitation I had placed upon myself based on one bad experience with one stressed-out teacher. It was the beginning of the identity "writer" and the suspension of the identity "artist" for quite some time. It was a Self I needed to remember, comfort and love. That teacher had made art class feel like math class to me. It wasn't until decades later that I dared to take another art class.

An Interview with Kellie Carbone
Psychotherapist, Mother and Writer
www.justtherapy.org
kelliecarbone@gmail.com

A fellow writer and client and later friend of mine, Kellie Carbone, had a similar experience being judged. In her case it was disguised as a question: "Who do you think you are?" She and I talked about the complexities of this question during our interview in 2010. Who asks it of us? When and what does it really mean, as we grow into who we become?

Kellie is originally from Michigan but lived in the San Francisco Bay Area for fifteen years, before she and her husband returned to Michigan in order to raise their young daughter and live closer to family. Kellie is petite with brown hair and fair skin. She is a generous and loving woman, and her green eyes show the kind of compassion forged through pain and perspective.

I began our interview with the question, "So who do you think you are?"

We both chuckled, and then she replied, "I think when that question is asked of us, usually the context is that you have stepped out of bounds, and others are questioning your right to take up space. The intent is to shut you down, send you back into silence, to make you think you don't have a right to be that person." Kellie elaborated, "It was said to me whenever I was playing with a new idea or identity. They said this out of fear."

"Your parents?" I asked, looking up from my notes. "Teachers?"

She nodded and added, "I think this question implies that you're being arrogant, too big for your britches. It's demeaning, a way to make you feel it wasn't okay to feel bigger."

"Why is it such a loaded question?" I asked. "Or is it really a statement or judgment?"

Kellie explained, "The reason it holds weight is the threat to the relationship. I remember thinking, as a child, that I would lose my parents or be abandoned or unloved. It speaks to that relational piece." She paused as she shifted her position on the sofa to get more comfortable. "They're going to stop loving us, but they're worried at the same time that we'll stop loving them."

"Are relationships more important to women and girls?" I wondered out loud. "Or is it that we're socialized to value relationships more than other aspects of our lives?"

Kellie nodded and said, "I think we have an internal conflict about outdoing or surpassing our mothers. I have to surrender the fear of losing my mother."

I added, "When people say, 'Who do you think you are?' in a judging way, Oprah says that what they really mean is, 'Who do you think I'm not?' They are threatened by your willingness to take risks or are jealous of your success."

She agreed, "When someone tells you that you can't do something, what it really means is that they can't do something, and they're afraid of trying."

"So how do we get beyond the fear, envy and judgment of 'Who do you think you are?'" I asked.

Kellie smiled and sat upright, before replying, "Sometimes I want to answer that question directly. Don't take it as a challenge you have to back down from, but take it as an invitation."

"To explore who you are?" I added and asked again, grinning, "So, who do you think you are, Kellie?"

She paused for a moment, considering her response. "While it's important to answer that question, we also need to leave space for not knowing. A better question might be, 'Who do you think you serve?'"

"God? Humankind?" I asked. "Ourselves?"

She looked up and said clearly, "I am a healer. I am a teacher. But it's hard to get that critical voice out of your head. The critique stops when I'm able to clear it all out, all the doubt, insecurity and fear, then I feel extremely powerful. I am an extension of the goddess. I am a healing force, helping people to find their voices."

"Sometimes our thoughts are incorrect and need adjustment," I agreed. "Often overly critical thoughts that stop us from achieving what we want are from past experiences with shame or guilt. As adults we need to find ways to heal ourselves."

As the mother of a two-year-old daughter at the time, Kellie ended our interview with a clear understanding of the challenges of parenting and not repeating the patterns that could harm her growing daughter. "I really have to surrender my ego and let her be who she's going to be." Kellie explained. "I constantly have to remind myself it's not about me. I can teach her and guide her, but she has her own life and path." I nodded as Kellie concluded, "What I really want to ask my daughter is, 'I see who you're becoming; who do you want to be?'"

This is an insightful question that we can also ask ourselves when we decide to figure out who we are. It is at the heart of transition and transformation, because who we think we are allows or limits our ability to become who we want to be.

Who Do You Think You Are? Explorations:

If you have 5 to 15 minutes, answer the following:

Who are you, really?

Who do you want to be?

Do you share that authentic you with everyone or just a few people? Why?

List several of your strengths and/or weaknesses here.

How often do you have an opportunity to express these parts of yourself?

Which aspects feel more comfortable and real to you? Why?

Which would you like to enhance and which would you prefer to decrease? Why?

Would you like to "try on" different aspects of your personality?

Who can best support you in doing that?

If you have more time, consider doing the following exploration:

Who we think we are is a construction of our perceptions and beliefs, based upon past experiences and present judgments. "Who are you?" We never get this question at parties. Instead we're asked, "What do you do?" We can discover, uncover and recover the lost remnants of ourselves and, from awareness, choose whom we want to become. Moreover, instead of just thinking, we can also feel who we are, allowing our emotions and sensations to align with our emerging sense of Self.

You have undertaken a brave and exciting adventure in seeking out the Self. You may wish to journal, collage or compose on the computer this exploration. You may also wish to collect items from storage, a collection or buy one or two new items for this project.

Today consider creating an altar to your essential Self. Altars were used in ancient times to honor the gods and the deceased. They do not have to be religious. Altars are still placed in homes and sacred spaces around the world for a variety of reasons. Clear a tabletop or bureau in your bedroom or office at home, place a tablecloth or scarf in your favorite color(s) over the surface and create an altar to remember and honor your true Self. You can include items from the past and present, gifts from others or yourself on your Self-altar. You can include a candle or incense to light daily, if you like, or items representing the five elements: fire, water, metal, earth and air.

For your Self-altar, also include objects that have special meaning for you: photographs, jewelry, keepsakes, mementos, a journal, whatever you want, just as long as it represents your true Self. You may find that this altar and the objects upon it will change over time, just as you will change. Do not be afraid to update it as you update yourself. Keep your Self-altar tidy and clear of dust and cobwebs. After all, it is a representation of you. Put away any object that no longer holds meaning for you. You can also place items on the altar that represent the person you'd like to become in the future. For example, if you want to learn how to dance, place dancing shoes on your altar. You can also create a wish or prayer box to place on your Self-altar into which you can place pieces of paper with wishes or prayers written on them.

Most importantly, have fun with it! This is your Self-altar. You can do anything you want with it.

Setting Intention, Choosing Priorities and Visualizing Goals©:

This self-exploration offers a quick way to prioritize your time in order to match your ideal priorities and purpose. ~20-30 minutes

1. Think about the most important aspects of your life. Then assess how many hours per week do you typically devote to the following categories? We each have only 24 hours a day, 7 days a week. How do you spend your time?

<u>Areas in life</u>

<u>Estimated # of hours per week</u>
(Total hours in a week = 24 x 7= 168 but don't worry too much about making the hours add up exactly.)

Family: spouse/children/pets
_____

Extended family
_____

Work
_____

Commute
_____

Errands/Housework/Cleaning/Repairs
_____

Fitness/Exercise/Sports
_____

Friends
_____

Hobbies
_____

Entertainment
_____

Spiritual pursuits
_____

Volunteer work/Charity
_____

Self-care
_____

Eating
_____

Rest/Sleep
_____

Other (Note: this could include emotions such as anxiety or behaviors such as daydreaming or planning):

2. Taking this list into consideration, how might you change these time commitments to be more in line with your ideal life? Which areas would you cut back on? Which areas would you expand? *Imagine that you could do anything you want to at this point. Don't hold yourself back with any concerns other than what your ideal life could be.*

Areas to cut back on:

Areas to expand:

This list will show your ideal priorities or what is actually most important to you. Does your ideal priorities list match up with your current time priorities? Why or why not? *Notice that whatever you tend to spend more time on than you would prefer robs you of the time you could devote to other priorities.*

3. Now it's time to consider in more detail *why* you haven't cut back or expanded on the areas of your life that you really want to. What keeps you from making changes in your life that would align more closely to your ideal life? Here are a few reasons some people have given in the past. Check off the ones that you believe apply to you. What other reasons might be holding you back?

___ Ego
___ Fear
___ Not feeling worthy
___ Pleasing others
___ Not certain what you want in life
___ Money
___ Time
___ Status
___ Obligation (to whom?_____)
___ Children
___ Other: _____
___ Other: _____
___ Other: _____

4. Who in your life would be willing or able to help you implement your action plan? Consider spouse, friends, mentors, counselor, clergy, acquaintances, boss, colleagues, others? Should you ask for help or do something on your own? Who are your role models? Whom do you admire who you can ask for advice about living a better life in alignment with your ideal priorities and life purpose?

5. Now that you have these lists in mind, ask yourself the following questions:

What specific steps could I take to bring my current time priorities more in line with my ideal life? Give yourself adequate time to implement an action plan. You don't have to complete everything all at once. You may have ideas that occur to you later in the days or weeks ahead. For now, write down at least one idea for each of the following:

What specific steps could I take to bring my current time priorities more in line with my ideal life?
Right now?

Over the next week?

Over the next month?

Over the next year?

Improving Relationships

The Blame Game

It is the enemy who can truly teach us to practice the virtues of compassion and tolerance.
–His Holiness the Dalai Lama

Who's to Blame?

We all have no doubt experienced times when we were blamed by another person or blamed someone else for a mistake or misunderstanding. It's human nature to want to feel good about ourselves, to want to believe the best about our own motives and actions and, thus, to discount, disown and project the parts of ourselves that we do not feel good about onto others. When we are this deeply unconscious of our motives, one unhealthy solution is to blame someone else for our mistakes, missteps or poor choices or to passively claim, like many politicians do, that: "Mistakes were made."

The blame game has no winners, only whiners.

The truth is that we are each responsible for our own thoughts, words and actions. We are never responsible for someone else's, even if they are our children (though it is possible to guide them toward better choices). One thought leads to a word or an action, then another and another. It is vital, therefore, to be mindful of our intentions. One practice I have personally found to be helpful is *vipassana*, mindfulness meditation.

Mindfulness Meditation

I first discovered *vipassana* when I was a stressed-out overachiever, working at an art museum as a full-time volunteer coordinator in 1997. I signed up for a stress reduction class, which was taught by a dentist, incidentally, who had been successfully using meditation with his patients in order to help alleviate pain. My first class, noticing my body and breath, was *not* a peaceful one. I was hyperventilating. I felt faint and nauseated, and I was shaking and crying uncontrollably. The rest of the people in the room seemed blissful. One guy even fell asleep! I realized in that brief moment of awareness that something in my life was terribly wrong. I wasn't so sure I was ready to find out what it was, but I kept going back.

Even though I was enrolled in this twelve-week class for stress reduction, it was not until some weeks later that I realized I had never let myself fully feel the grief of losing my maternal grandfather and my paternal grandmother, who had passed away within a few months of each other. I had instead blamed a heavy workload and a highly competitive atmosphere at work. We were gearing up for the museum's reopening in 1997, after a decade of closure due to the 1989 Loma Prieta earthquake, during which the museum buildings required earthquake retrofit construction. I had also blamed the petty gossip of two of my co-workers for my distress. They were mean. They told lies about me. They also would never confront me directly, so I could discuss issues openly with them and find a way to resolve our differences. It was always a stab in the back, a nasty rumor or a "joke" that I just didn't have the sophistication or skill to deflect yet. They were young women, like myself, who were doing the best they could, climbing up from the low end of the non-profit ladder. For a time, it was easier for me to focus on the petty surface issues than to confront the real wound: a gaping hole of loss and sorrow, with which I had not had the time, space or ability to cope.

    I later went to a counselor on campus, and she helped me to see the depth of my grief, blame and victimhood, feelings of loss that echoed experiences in my childhood that were not yet resolved. I asked my boss for a long weekend off (thinking it was too much, when actually it was too little time off). During that time away I discovered I had a variety of choices I hadn't considered before. I rearranged my schedule when I came back, so that I did not have to be around the difficult co-workers, or I wore earplugs when our schedules overlapped, so I wouldn't have to overhear their spiteful words. I focused on what was important and got the job done, until I could gather the courage to confront these co-workers, train my successor and leave with dignity.

Clarity about Taking Personal Responsibility vs. Blaming Others

One of the lessons I learned from this experience was how we can convince ourselves that another person deserves pain or suffering, that they have somehow brought it upon themselves. I hated these young women for the additional pain I felt they were unfairly inflicting upon me during that difficult time, and I wished them grievous harm. They, in turn, probably picked up on my anger and felt they had a right to fight back. Like myself, these two young women had been assigned to answer the non-stop doorbell for guests whenever it rang, even if we were in the middle of a project deadline, whereas the curators and other staff could ignore the bell. We only had Master's degrees, and the PhDs trumped that, along with their seniority and higher positions. It wasn't just the constant interruptions were annoying, but rather, the assumption that we, as "lower-level" staff, should be treated as doormen. To be clear, I didn't mind answering the door, rather I minded the assumption that it should be my duty to do so, superseding my other responsibilities.

Our department was not alone in this hierarchical mode of operation. The university's employee survey that year posed the pertinent question, "How can we retain qualified staff?" The fact that employee retention was an issue was an indicator of a serious problem. There is a fine line between assigning duties that need to be completed versus treating people as underlings. Fortunately, in meditation, I realized that everyone else concerned was also suffering and that the problem was an institutional one that I could not change on my own.

What I could do, however, was to use the techniques I had learned in the mindful meditation class. Whenever I felt myself overwhelmed or upset, I would remember to breathe to center myself and notice my thoughts. I would remember that my thoughts and feelings, though functional and human, were not necessarily the "Truth." Rather, they were merely my perceptions of a truth. I noticed how my body felt, and I ate when I was hungry, drank when I was thirsty and slept when I was tired. I remembered to be kind to myself, and, as a result, I also found that I could be kinder to others, even the women who were being unkind to me. I found I had choices, powerful choices, about how and where, when and why I could interact and impact others. I was awake to the fact that others also acted or reacted based upon their own perceptions of "reality," which could be vastly different from my own perceptions. Most importantly, I discovered my beliefs about situations and people were not necessarily true and that it was wise to notice and respect this newfound awareness, without buying into the stories I was telling myself. A few months later, being aware of what I wanted and what I was willing to accept, I found a better job teaching English as a Second Language, where I was more appreciated and paid a better salary.

The blame game is a double-edged sword

The blame game is a double-edged sword. One might feel justified being the "innocent" victim, rather than a neutral participant or a wrongdoer, but it leaves you helpless and at the mercy of others who "do unto" you. By blaming others for our pain, we suffer and complain ineffectively, instead of taking action to change the situation or our reactions to it. The blame game leaves us and the people we blame completely disempowered, instead of offering opportunities for self-reflection, positive action and transformation. By becoming more aware, realizing we have choices and acting in alignment with our better selves, we can change our minds, hearts and world for the better.

The Blame Game Exploration:

If you have 5 to 10 minutes, answer the following:

Who has blamed you for something in your life?

How did you feel about this? What did you do about it?

Have you blamed someone else? Who? Why?

Has the blame game served you in the past? How? Why?

Are you ready to take complete responsibility for your own thoughts, words and actions?

If you have more time, do the following explorations:

Are you willing to let your "story" go and to take charge of your own choices and experiences?

Awareness is the key to behavior. If you are not yet ready to take responsibility for your own thoughts and actions, ask yourself why?

What are the obstacles preventing you from taking charge of your own life?

If you are ready, make a list of empowering thoughts, words and actions you can take instead of blaming, disempowering ones.

Past disempowering belief(s)   Present empowering action(s)

Write on a piece of paper: "I am responsible for my own thoughts, words and actions. I take back my power, and I know that I can change the circumstances of my own life. I choose to forgive _____ for their choices, and I will find a way to make something positive come from this experience."

Make a blame game collage. Use this statement and any magazine and catalog images, artwork and any visual representations of the experience of blame to illustrate how it feels to be trapped in the illusion of the blame game.

Then set yourself free. Rip it to pieces, burn it in effigy or transform it into another collage that more accurately reflects your conscious choice to reclaim your own power, presence and freewill.

Reality Check

What you get by achieving your goals is not as important as what you become by achieving your goals.
–Henry David Thoreau

Really Reality?

The most important moment of my life was when I realized that I create meaning from everything occurring around me.

I was suffering a great deal about a situation over which I had no control. I was in love with someone who was not in love with me. It had happened to me in college, over twenty years earlier, and it was more about my own need for love than it was about the other person's lack of it for me.

The object of my affection was a truly extraordinary man, boyishly charming yet also ambitious, humorous and humble, commanding and yet compassionate. He was everything I wanted in a man. Problem was, he did not love me. I sobbed. I commiserated with my girlfriends. I had doubts about my beauty, sense of humor and intelligence. I was in despair, or so I thought, until I realized that what I was actually suffering from was that I did not want to accept reality as it was in that moment. I believed he didn't love me. Moreover, I believed it was because of some shortcoming in myself, something I needed to change or make up for, which was completely untrue. In truth his not loving me had nothing to do with me at all. My not loving myself enough to find someone else who could love me was the real issue.

Events occur, people are who they are, but the meaning I make of anything is up to me.

There are moments over and over again in my life when I forget who I am. From time to time, I still falsely believe that the answers are somewhere outside of myself, in the love of someone beside myself or in some action or reward outside of myself. However, I am getting better at recognizing when this occurs, what triggers it and can choose to shift my thoughts.

What Reality is Real?

Some people look to others for advice or guidance, which is fine, as long as they do not give over their power to a leader, healer or guru, thinking that the other person has all the answers they are seeking. Many people pray to God for support and help in times of trouble. Nothing is wrong with that, but we often forget that the truth, our Truth, is within us. God/dess is always within us.

When we're looking for answers outside of ourselves, it's about projection: superimposing your feelings or thoughts or beliefs onto someone else. The danger with projection is that it leaves you feeling helpless, alone and incapable of changing your present or future. It puts your power in other people's hands, and it keeps you stuck in what-ifs. As Carl Jung, once said in "The Symbolic Life," a seminar talk given in 1939 to the Guild for Pastoral Psychology in London, "… It is the hallucination of loneliness, and it is a loneliness that cannot be quenched by anything else. You can be a member of a society with a thousand members, and you are still alone. That thing in you which should live is alone; nobody touches it, nobody knows it, you yourself don't know it; but it keeps on stirring, it disturbs you, it makes you restless, and it gives you no peace."[5] This kind of delusional thinking keeps you locked up in a box of your own imagining, lonely and neurotic.

So, to return to my earlier dilemma, years later, I realized that my illusory lover would not love me back, not because I was unlovable or unworthy of love, but because he simply did not love me. Furthermore, he later told me that he wasn't really sure what love was. He had loved another woman, and when they finally broke up, it had left him numb, exhausted and, understandably, cautious. When I loved him, he wasn't able to do more than concentrate on his studies and work. Another relationship, with its inherent emotional demands and obligations, would have been too much. But even if he had been able to return my love, it was simply not meant to be. The reality of the situation was that I could choose to suffer, wishing things were different, trying to prove I was "worthy," or accept reality, knowing I was worthy of my own love and move forward. He did not love me, but I could love myself. Someday someone else would love me.

An Interview with Martina Ashanti
U Gotta Love Yourself (U.G.L.Y.) Attitude Initiative and Imagine Mentoring LLC

http://imaginementoring.com/
DomesticVictor@gmail.com

My former client and dear friend Martina Ashanti is a remarkable woman. She converted to Islam in her twenties, and she approaches that religion with an empowering feminist perspective. She has worked for many years with young women, and in 2008, with her best friend Christian Nicole, she co-formed a non-profit in the Detroit area entitled U.G.L.Y., an acronym for the U Gotta Love Yourself Attitude Initiative. Later in L.A. she continued to offer workshops and support groups to at-risk young women. She now works with Imagine Mentoring LLC in Detroit. Martina is slender and yet strong, like a willow tree. She is a mother of two young daughters, and she has had her own challenges with reality checks.

First Interview with Martina Ashanti, April 20, 2009

Lani: So you were saying that in 2005, you saw a quote by Eleanor Roosevelt that really stood out to you, "The future belongs to those who believe in the beauty of their dreams." Maybe talk about some of the dreams you have for what you're creating, you mentioned a clothing line and you're working on a video?

Martina: Yep. Video Production Associate's degree at Washtenaw Community College. It's really exciting. I have a lot of people that have assisted me, especially now, and many times I don't always know it, you know, but they're there to offer their help. They don't always know just how much they've touched my life.

Lani: And it's true that we also serve that role. I think God, Spirit, what have you, works through us when we're open to that.

Martina: Yes.

Lani: And it's amazing what connections will happen and synchronicities. You know, someone will say something or you'll say something to someone, and it really resonates with them.

Martina: Yeah, that's true. I'm sitting here reflecting.

Lani: It's powerful when that happens.

Martina: Very powerful. And it's in those moments, when you're at that point of transition, when you ask yourself, "Well, what am I going to do with the life that I have left?" And in that you're really asking yourself, "Who am I going to be in this life that I have left?" It's accepting life for what it is. You know, when you really don't know how important you are, how significant you are, when people are relying upon you to be who you are. It's a beautiful thing, it's a great thing if you are who you are, not apologizing for it, and be happy. My imperfections make me imperfect me, and that is okay. I can be uniquely different.

Lani: It's amazing that one person's imperfections are actually perfect for that situation. For example stubbornness, which is also perseverance.

Martina: We were all born to win. It definitely is a reeducation, discovering who you are, why you're here and what you created to be, just be, is an awesome thing.

Lani: And being open to the possibilities that come your way, aware of opportunities.

Martina: I can speak for myself when I say that for a large portion of my life, I pardoned what I knew to be true because others didn't get it. They didn't understand many things I was already aware of, but I downplayed or suppressed it a lot. But maybe, just maybe, if I was more confident, I would not downplay what I know to be true.

Lani: It sounds like a big shift occurred for you.

Martina: Yes, a huge shift. I'm more self-assured, more aware and more happy now. I wasn't content with just being. So I had to lose all of the other whos and whats, perceptions and beliefs, and say, you know what, no thank you. It's liberating. I feel so free. As a young girl, many young girls I know, they are searching for someone to give them permission; it's okay to be who you are. Be who you are. You're perfect. You're okay. It's fine. You'll do just fine. We need that reassurance. Once you have that confidence, that self-esteem, that reassurance, then you're content, and everything else falls into place.

Lani: What are some of the meanings that you took away from this awakening?

Martina: That I really didn't lose anything. That everything that I've experienced, that every pause, every play, every rewind, every fast-forward was kind of like a learning lesson. I was actually right on time. At that moment I was on purpose, and I was just gathering.

Lani: That's an awesome realization.

Martina: You think so?

Lani: Yes, because in that is the power to accept things as they are and not suffer.

Martina: Yeah.

Lani: Even if you're not feeling well, or you're feeling off, it's simply a day to rest. It's a time to take better care, instead of forging ahead. A lot of women in particular are trained to self-sacrifice at the expense of our well-being. It's not healthy, and it's not good for anyone else, either. It definitely makes so much more sense to love and care for oneself. We can then take better care of others, but even in and of itself, we matter and are worth taking care of ourselves.

Martina: We have to matter. Everyone else matters but us. That's such a perversion of why we're here.

Lani: Why does that happen? Do you think it's blindness or ignorance or discrimination?

Martina: I believe we are created to love thy neighbor as thyself, but we forget the thyself part. We sometimes lose ourselves in transition. In translating our love for others, we stop loving ourselves.

Lani: And some people haven't yet learned how to love themselves or others.

Martina: Yes, that's right.

Lani: How have your past experiences impacted who you are and who you want to be in the present?

Martina: It qualifies me to assist others. To reach my hand out to other people and say, "Hey, you know what, it's okay. I've been through the exact same thing. And guess what, you're going to rise to the occasion, and you're going to become all that you're created to become. You are being and doing what you were sent here to do. Everything that you are and will be is great."

Lani: Have you noticed that how we interpret our experience impacts the experience more than the experience itself? How we interpret our past lives in the present, impacts what we do, say or think in the future and influences what we think is possible. What would you say has been the most helpful to you, what experience or what belief has been the most helpful to you in terms of creating your life?

Martina: I believe that no matter what the Creator decrees for my life, it's always for the greater good, even beyond myself. If I experience a hurt, whether someone wrongs me or I wrong someone else, at the end of the day, it's always for the greater good. There's a spiritual benefit for us both and as a collective. So I don't hold grudges. At that moment it's forgiven and done with.

Lani: I often say a prayer, "Please let me act in the interests for the highest good of all, myself included."

Martina: That's a powerful prayer. This is the one time I've really had a chance to let go of all the past hurts.

Follow-up interviews via e-mail with Martina Ashanti, January 31 and August 12, 2013:

Lani: How have your views on loving oneself, in general, and self-love for women, specifically, changed over the past couple of years?

Martina: When I last interviewed with you in 2009, I was 27 years old. Every part of my being, life, work, personal and professional relationships illuminated the truth of who I was and what I believed and knew to be true. I say this to others, "You gotta love yourself." I say it to myself, "I love me." In May 2010, the platform that I stood on, my most intimate thoughts, beliefs, teachings and core of my being were being tested.

Lani: You have already shared with me how difficult that time was and how painful. I am glad we have stayed in touch. Would you mind sharing with the readers of this book what happened?

Martina: It was the beginning of a nightmare, where I endured words of poison, physical, emotional, sexual and mental abuse by my spouse. As a result, I lost my home, car, job, my personal and professional relationships were strained. I would work 10-16 hour days to escape the turmoil and still mentor and pour into the lives of others, while pregnant and enduring domestic violence.

I would think to myself, *How did I get into this mess? This is chaos. What am I to learn from this?*

Lani: You are not alone, sadly. According to the National Domestic Violence Hotline website:

> Domestic violence can happen to anyone of any race, age, sexual orientation, religion or gender. It can happen to couples who are married, living together or who are dating. Domestic violence affects people of all socioeconomic backgrounds and education levels.[6]

Domestic violence is about power and control of another person. It can happen to anyone. You are very brave to share this with us.

Martina: Reality check! Some people will see your light and be afraid to walk in their own truth and will fight you to the death to put a shade on your light. It was amazing to see another human being project their self-hate, past hurts and dissatisfaction with another person upon me. I had someone trying to convince me that I wasn't beautiful, that I was incompetent, unworthy of being who I am, unworthy of being loved, admired, protected and honored by him or others. In those moments, I felt powerless. I know now I have power because I always have a choice.

Lani: Yes. We always have choices, even in the darkest, scariest, loneliest times.

Martina: As a Domestic Victor [Note: Martina is currently developing a program for survivors of domestic violence called Domestic Victor®] over Domestic Violence, I can say today that I do love myself. My test was standing before someone who was a mirror of me, someone who would tirelessly project self-pity, anger and aggression. He tried to sell me the idea that I am not worthy of love, kindness, dignity or peace. When someone tries to project their toxic beliefs upon you, you have the choice to believe them and give them license to wreak havoc in your life, or you can send a clear message by what you say, where you spend your time, how you live your life, and the boundaries that you set to show that you do not agree with them.

Lani: Can you share with us how you managed to break free of the lies and this abuse?

Martina: Yes. The reality check for me was realizing that his opinions, negative views and assaultive behavior were not my reality. And so, I made a new choice. I ended the relationship. This was a teaching moment for me because I know in life, the only thing we have control over is ourselves. The energy and effort we put into trying to change others' lies, manipulation, coercion or abuse is better invested in improving ourselves.

Lani: Are you afraid to share your story at all? Is there anything I should leave out for your safety and the safety of your daughters?

Martina: Being a Domestic Victor is to live B.R.A.V.E. (Beyond Regrets Achieving Victories Everyday). Thank you for the love, prayers, light and mantle of protection. We love you and appreciate you handling us with care. He was incarcerated for a short stint and is wearing a GPS tether. Glory to the Almighty! All is now well over here.

Lani: I am so glad to hear that!

Martina: This is what happened. To maintain power and control, he tried to kill my daughter, Sadaqah, and me. Despite the personal protection order, pending court case, the abuse continued even in the company of his mother and family. For the record, none of his family condoned or tolerated his behavior. Yet, he sent a clear message to me that either I get with his program or suffer the consequences.

I knew the abuse was not going to stop, because he was not willing to accept any responsibility and change his violent behavior. I learned later that this was a part of the battering cycle. (http://www.helpguide.org) I knew that I had exhausted every option for us to be decent and co-parent for the welfare of our children. To break free, I came up with an escape plan. I stepped out on faith and never looked back.

Lani: What did you do? How did you plan your escape? Did you have help along the way?

Martina: I remember driving by myself from California cross-country, three-months pregnant and with six-month-old Sadaqah, for our freedom. No one knew of my plan until I took action. There were times when I didn't have all the answers or resources. It was a small and mighty alliance of people that helped us along the way. My parents and four families in particularly really protected us. Also, there were some great organizations that helped: ILM Foundation (www.ilmercy.com), Al-Maun Fund (www.almaunfund.org) and United Way 2-1-1 (http://www.211.org). By the mercy of God, the kindness of a few strangers, support of close friends and the stability of family, Sadaqah, Hidayah and I are here today.

Lani: Not only did you take steps and take action to create a better life for you and your daughters, but you had to change the beliefs and thoughts that someone else was trying to impose on you. You also had to have the courage to reach out to the appropriate people for help. What advice do you have for others going through something similar?

Martina: You will always have the power, because in life you have a choice. Loving yourself by making healthy decisions that serve your greatest good is real power. The most meaningful decision that anyone can make in their lives is to love themselves. We spend every waking hour with ourselves, so we should be dutifully committed, confident and content with who we are. We should never be willing to make ourselves accommodate someone who is not willing to do their own work or honor and be good to themselves.

Lani: It is a brave and difficult choice to leave. A lot of people don't understand that batterers tend to grind their victims down. They use abusive words, financial and social isolation, fear and uncertainty and/or physical and sexual assault until the survivor's self-esteem is practically non-existent. Sometimes families are not supportive of a survivor leaving, though I know your family was. Thank you so much for your courage and generosity in sharing your experience and empowering choice with us.

Martina: Peace & Love Lani! Thank you for allowing me to share this opportunity and good works with you!

Lani: You're welcome and thank you! Speaking of empowering choices, could you tell us more about the U.G.L.Y Initiative and the work you and Christian Nicole do with Imagine Mentoring in Detroit, Michigan? http://www.http://imaginementoring.com/

Martina: Sure. The U.G.L.Y. (U Gotta Love Yourself) Attitude Initiative is a labor of love for my best friend Christian Nicole and me. The Initiative began as a platform to remind people to love themselves, stop apologizing and embrace who they are. The program is designed to serve at-risk youth and young adults with tools that enable them to accept themselves, live by core values, enhance their skills and use their knowledge to lead with love, confidence, character and purpose. We strongly believe in preserving humanity through service and community outreach. We have now partnered with I.M.A.G.I.N.E. Mentoring LLC in Detroit to assist in completing these projects and missions.

Lani: Fabulous! It sounds like you have truly found your calling. In addition to work outside the home, you are also a mom, which is also an important calling. Now that you have daughters, how do you instill a sense of self worth in them and in yourself?

Martina: To instill a sense of self-worth in my family, I live a life of truthful expression, setting boundaries and making healthy decisions that reflect the love, peace and happiness that resonates from within and extends outward. My daughters are my miracles from God. In Arabic, Sadaqah means "Charity," and Hidayah means "God's Guidance." They remind me that they are love, I am loved and we need each other. Every decision I make is with them in mind. I am conscious of our diet. We are now surrounded by positive people who believe in us. The more honest, open and mindful we make the environment that we share with our children, the more we enable our children to be resilient and to move confidently and independently into this world with love.

Lani: Finally, I want to ask, what are some steps you take to love yourself every day?

Martina: Every action I make in my life is affirming that I love myself, and I am giving gratitude and paying homage to the Creator, Maintainer and Sustainer of Life. The Originating Source. My guide post is Al-Islam. I strive to be in peaceful practice everyday. The decisions that I make affirm that I know and live a life that is best for me. I am worthy and valuable beyond human comprehension. I am validated in truth by those actions and decisions that I make, that I am love. Neither the media, society, my past mistakes/learning experiences or poor self-opinion of others will convince me otherwise.

So I use my money as a tool to fulfill my commitments and give to charity to ease the hardship for others. I pray, quiet my spirit to realign and get insight from The Creator. It's like washing your hands and taking a shower every day, cleansing of the soul. I read, watch and listen to positive, nourishing information that improves my quality of life. I am available and willing to serve; be it a smile, kind word or a helping hand. I tell the truth! I'm truthful about my expectations, who I am as a person, my values, opinions, personal and professional struggles. I embrace flaws and all. I strive to improve myself every day. In loving myself, I experience life on a day-to-day basis. All is well here.

Lani: I am so glad you are safe, encouraging others and thriving! Mahalo for sharing your story. I wish more people realized that they can change their lives for the better if they believe they can, then reach out for appropriate support from others and take active steps to make it happen. I know you will inspire many survivors to seek help and support. They can contact the National Domestic Violence Hotline at 1–800–799–SAFE (7233) or TTY 1–800–787–3224 for more information.

The Epiphany

Martina and I both realized we could continue to create our own suffering by holding onto fantasies that would never come true, that other people would change, or we could choose to learn from these experiences and move on with compassion for ourselves and others. We could remain stuck in an obsession, or we could let it go and remember that everything is in Divine order. Even if it was not yet clear to us that there would be benefits to these early heartbreaks, events occur and other people are who they are, but we each get to choose the meanings we create from these experiences. From every situation there is something to gain, if we can remain open-minded and open-hearted.

It wasn't until years later that I read a book by therapist and relationship expert Katherine Woodward Thomas. In *Calling in "the One": Seven Weeks to Attract the Love of Your Life*, she writes in reply to a client who wondered if she would ever heal:

> I don't know that we ever 'get rid' of our woundedness. Our wounding experiences are a part of our history. We can, however, give up defining ourselves by what happened to us in the past. We can stop identifying with the pain that we have suffered. This is not a denial of what we've been through but, rather, an awareness that the essence of who we are is far, far beyond it.[7]

Reading this was, to quote Oprah, an "A-ha! Moment" for me. I shared this quote and the book with my friend Martina, and she agreed, a past built remembering pain without also valuing the lessons we have learned and the strength we have gained is not the way either of us would ever choose to live.

Later we would see beyond the exterior situation to the interior core of the problem: our own false beliefs that the situations were a problem. The situations simply were what they were. Reality check. What we learned was that the meaning we take away from any and all experiences is completely up to us. We can consciously choose how each moment impacts us, regardless of whether or not other people behave as we wish they would or whether or not events go according to our plans. We can allow life to unfold as it will, focusing on the true love that always exists within each of us—an aware acceptance of Self and of others.

Reality Check Explorations:

If you have 5 to 10 minutes, answer the following:

Have you ever had a situation in your life that didn't go according to your plan? If so, what was it?

Looking back on that experience now, list all the things you learned about yourself and/or other people.

If you have more time, answer the following:

Look beyond what was painful and ask yourself, "What was helpful in this reality check?" What do you know now that you didn't know then?

What would you tell another person whom you cared about who was going through something similar? Now take that advice for yourself.

Is Your Glass Half Full or Half Empty?

The only thing more irresistible than telling the truth is listening to it. Like moths drawn to the flame, we flit through our entire lives secretly searching for stolen moments when we can allow ourselves to be swept away by something larger than the life we've settled for.
–Sarah Ban Breathnach, *Something More: Excavating Your Authentic Self*

Seeing the Glass Half Full or Half Empty?

Seeing the glass as half full or half empty is a well-known representation used to illustrate whether a person tends to be optimistic or pessimistic. Yet, in reality, our symbolic glasses are half full and half empty at the same time. Both states exist, unless our glass is completely empty or full to the brim, and that varies from moment to moment.

Each person's "truth" is filtered through their own past experiences and present sensations, feelings and thoughts. Truth with a capital "T" is an objective reality filtered through multiple lenses to create multiple narratives woven together, as in a novel with different narrators. An event occurs, but different people will have different perspectives on the Truth. So, the only way to know the Truth fully, or at least a fuller more objective Truth (if you are brave and honest enough to actually want to know it), is to be willing to share your own truth and listen and try to understand another person's truth.

What is the "Truth" with a capital "T"?

Recently, I have been asking my sisters about their childhood experiences to see if they mesh with my own. I am the eldest of three girls. We were born in three different states—Georgia, Florida and California—within a year or two of each other. My father was in the U.S. Navy and was a 2nd class petty officer stationed on the U.S.S. Hancock, an aircraft carrier, off the northern coast of Vietnam during these early years of our lives. My mother became pregnant each time he was home on leave, hence the three relocations near Naval bases in Georgia, Florida and California during that time. Then when I was three, the entire family picked up and moved to the island of Oʻahu.

I remember that my mother was often deeply unhappy. She tried her best to care for us, but I now believe that she was suffering from anxiety and depression. She was later diagnosed with agoraphobia, the fear of being around other people. In part this was inherited. Her mother, Grandma Temple, had suffered tremendous loss and deprivation during the Great Depression and had been hospitalized on numerous occasions for what was then termed a "nervous breakdown." My great-grandmother had also fallen into depression when her husband left her to raise a family on her own. Grandma Temple remembered many times when her family did not have enough to eat. My Grandpa Temple's family owned their own bar and were farmers, so they were not impacted as badly by the Depression. However, there was trauma, pain and poverty faced by both sides of that family. It was an era when people did not get therapy. There used to be a stigma associated with mental illness. Instead people did their best to keep it to themselves, hide and deny it, which, of course, makes situations like these much worse.

My father was away much of the time during the Vietnam

War. Later, when the war was over, he was often at work, putting in overtime as a mechanic at the U.S. Army installation at Schofield Barracks and later at Pearl Harbor Naval Base, leaving my mother home alone with three young children. My father must have felt overwhelmed at times, too. Perhaps he had undiagnosed PTSD or depression? He would go out for a drink on Fridays with his buddies from work and, sometimes, he wouldn't come home all weekend, saying he never wanted his children to see him drunk. He never spoke with us directly about it. We got all this secondhand from Mom, who had reasons to be angry with him and tended to be the kind of person who held grudges.

My father's mother had also coped with depression during a time in which this mental illness was misunderstood. During World War II her beloved eldest brother was interred for being a journalist with a Japanese-language newspaper. This was no doubt deeply painful and embarrassing to her, and she never really got over it. Grandpa Kwon coped in other ways, though it is highly controversial in the 'ohana as to whether he was really an alcoholic or not. He was definitely a workaholic or merely hardworking, depending upon whom you ask. Grandpa and Grandma Kwon both did their best to assimilate into middle class America and never spoke about the war or subsequent years, when Grandma Kwon also suffered a nervous breakdown. All of them were wounded but in different ways.

I remember my sisters and I comforting Mom, holding her as she sobbed like a child, saying, "It's going to be okay," but not knowing if this was really true. I felt helpless. As the eldest I felt responsible for looking after her, my sisters and myself from a very early age. I sometimes resented it and rebelled by hiding in the cliffside caves near where we lived in Makakilo. Most of the time I just coped the best way I could.

Fortunately, my sister Lea and I got along, and we were

able to survive together, as a surrogate mother and father to our parents and youngest sister. Lea has similar memories to mine. She was the middle child, nine going on thirty-nine. When I asked her what she remembered specifically about that time, she e-mailed me the following on January 27, 2013:

> Mom definitely suffered from depression, as well as agoraphobia, panic attacks, and I believe she said her doctor thought she had PTSD from all the worry when Dad would disappear.
>
> The depression was caused by a combination of money problems, being unhappy with Dad and being socially isolated in a culture she didn't really understand. It had to be hard to be an overweight, shy, *haole* (Caucasian). Mom hated living in Hawai'i.
>
> When I heard that Dante quote in school about making a 'hell out of heaven,' I instantly thought of Mom, since most people would love to live in 'paradise'. The panic attacks made Mom agoraphobic, since she was afraid that she would have one when she was in public. That's actually pretty common.
>
> I recall being woken up many times in the middle of the night, when I was in maybe 5th or 6th grade, when Mom was having a panic attack and having to calm her down. Not sure if she ever did that to you guys. Also having to handle grocery shopping etc... when Mom couldn't leave the house.
>
> Hope this is helpful.[8]

She remembers being responsible for folding laundry, doing dishes, grocery shopping, taking care of my mother and making sure our youngest sister, Laura, combed her hair, brushed her teeth, put on clean clothes and was ready for school. It was not an easy time for us.

Laura remembers things differently. She used to complain about her older sisters teasing her, getting her in trouble and telling her what to do. She did not respond to my request for her memories of this time in our childhood.

Growing up, I also remember watching reruns of old sitcoms and sci-fi television shows with my mother and sisters. In fact I barely remember a moment when the T.V. wasn't on. We loved how everything was fixed, happily-ever-after and concluded within a half hour episode. I vividly remember one episode of the original *Star Trek* entitled "The Empath."[9] In this episode a female healer is coerced by big-brained aliens to heal the doctor, Bones, against her will. She had the ability to take on others' pain, but at a high cost to herself. I remember being pissed off by that as a child, resentful that anyone thought they had a right to impose their will on someone else and that this healer had to get sick so that someone else could get well. I remember Mom had a different take. She thought it was the highest calling to serve through self-sacrifice. So you can see, this was confusing to me at age eight or nine. My naturally healthy boundaries were crossed many times, and there was not much I could do about it as a child.

Bias: Does It Wash Both Ways?

A friend of mine once gave me an excellent piece of advice, "You can always tell if something is biased," he said. "Just ask yourself, 'Does it wash both ways?'" Would the aliens have supported the idea of the male characters sacrificing themselves in this way for the woman? I doubt it. Was my mother there for her own mother in the same way she expected her daughters to be there for her? Probably. Would she have expected the same from a son? Maybe. And what of my father? Why was he not held accountable? Did all this happen before or after I was sexually assaulted by acquaintances of my parents? And did that event contribute to the breakdown in the family, or was the family already dysfunctional? I don't know.

That is what I do not remember. The sequence of events is

cloudy. Memories are clear in some instances and fragmented or completely missing in others. That's what trauma does. In my experience I have discovered that the mind, body and heart contain and buffer extremely painful moments in order to help us survive them. We sometimes forget in order to forgive. Yet healing, for me, is the process of remembering accurately and then creating a new story, a version of my own truth. Was I a victim or survivor? Was I wounded or a healer who heals others by taking on their pain or maybe someone who can bear witness to others' pain without taking on their suffering, too? Am I broken or mended or capable of supporting others in their own healing work? That's where my power is, in my ability to choose…now that I am all grown up.

So, what matters is how we choose to interpret the experiences that we encounter in life, the meanings that we make from these incidents and, finally, whether or not we learn how to refill our own glasses and the glasses of others by seeing situations as they are, while also maintaining hope for a better future. Years later, in an episode of *Star Trek: The Next Generation* entitled "Man of the People,"[10] a similar situation unfolds, where an ambassador uses empathic Counselor Troi by placing all of his hate, fear and other unpleasant emotions into her, as if she is a container for his dark side. However, this time, Captain Picard will not stand for Deanna Troi being used in this way. In the thirty odd years between the original series and the Next Generation, my mother's generation and my own, women have become valued as individuals. This is significant and a cultural shift, due in large part to the women's movement and feminism. We are who we are in any given set of circumstances and scenarios. Yet, we create our own realities by how we translate, interpret and, in some cases, replay or even edit the events, sensations and interactions in our lives.

This practice is not always a wise one. There are times

when, as the familiar saying goes, "Ignorance is bliss." Any time there is a situation that could be harmful or dangerous to you or others, steer clear, stand strong in your own truth and allow others to have their own truth. For example, if revealing a hidden truth may cause another person to commit suicide or murder, it may be wise to consider whether or not to share it publicly. However, if objectivity will help you to heal a past wound, transgression or deep sorrow, I encourage you to ask someone else involved if his or her truth matches your own. Seek sources of support, such as a therapist, minister, family member or close friend you trust who will listen without judgment.

Be open to other people's truths. Be willing to see things from another point of view. Be willing to be surprised.

An Interview with Amy Garber
Spiritual Counselor, Psychic Channel and Medium
http://www.metafizz.org

I first met Amy Garber through the Interfaith Center for Spiritual Growth in Ann Arbor, Michigan. Amy emanates a peaceful, yet focused energy. She has dark shoulder-length hair and a twinkle in her brown eyes. She has worked in PR and marketing for years and is also an intuitive counselor, teacher and channel. Amy first attended one of my workshops when she was experiencing a job-related transition, and we later became friends and fellow writers in a writing group. She was featured on a 2013 episode of *House Hunters* on HGTV, providing intuitive guidance to a woman seeking a home. http://www.annarbor.com/entertainment/hgtvs-house-hunters-to-feature-ann-arbor-monday-night/ I first interviewed her in 2009 about how life transitions can be an opportunity for growth, healing and perspective and then followed up with her in 2013.

Lani: You, like many people, have been through incredibly difficult times in your life. I'm grateful for this time together and your willingness to share your experiences with others about your fiancé Larry's diagnosis and transition when he passed away and other transitions in your life.

Amy: It's important to have faith and optimism and view the glass as half full even when going through an ordeal like my fiancé's cancer. I still feel the six months we did have were much better because we focused on hope and optimism.

Lani: So there's a choice even in things you don't think you have a choice about?

Amy: Yes, your attitude and your thoughts really play a role in life. I guess I'm also the type of person who leaves no stone unturned, and then I knew that at least I had done everything I could. And I wasn't alone, there were many people supporting us and offering help. People gave advice and support. Angels were placed to help us, and they were a constant source of encouragement.

Lani: It sounds as though it was also important to know that you can get through anything and that you didn't need to do it completely alone.

Amy: Yes. I know I made a conscious choice to make the best of things. I've also done this in relation to other events or choices in my life. For example, in my work, when I get to a certain point and I tried different tactics, I realize what debilitated me for a while was fear. I realized this fear was keeping me from going in and having a normal experience each day. I made the conscious choice to just surrender. As the Buddha has said, "The source of suffering is the resistance to what is."

Lani: So you made a conscious choice about how much you allowed fear to dominate your thoughts?

Amy: Yes. I needed to realize that I do not need to take negativity in. I let other people's behaviors bother me at work, when I started to believe the judgment of others. I realized I just needed to let go of it and focus on my own choices. Over and over again, I reminded myself that I knew I'd be okay, that the outcome I couldn't see yet is still something I can have faith in.

Lani: When you took part in the Creating CoPOWERment® Workshops, what sort of transition were you encountering?

Amy: I wanted to get a new job and was also struggling with a tense situation at my current job. I felt stressed much of the time. Either I felt I had no time to myself or, when I did, I had anxiety about what to do first.

Lani: What new approaches, connections and/or insights did you gain from your experience in the Creating CoPOWERment® Workshops?

Amy: What was interesting was that I thought the images I would choose in the vision board and the message I would get from the workshop would be guidance about a new job, but instead, everything I chose focused on inner peace and happiness! "Health," "simplify," "balance," "quality time," "harmony," "beauty" and "body, mind spirit" were the sayings that I cut out from magazines with pictures to match. And, indeed, that was what I most needed to focus on at that time. Because of this awareness that your workshop gave me, I started a process of moving towards joy and release from stress and anxiety. I had the power to do this, and it was my choice! I truly believe that this is how I got through the following six months and was calm enough to make different choices and attract a new job.

Lani: What advice or guidance would you offer others going through a similar transition?

Amy: Doing an exercise like your "Ideal Priorities/Purpose Exploration" is invaluable in seeing where you currently are in your life, by what you spend your time on. It's a sobering realization when you see in black and white what you're giving your time to, especially compared to what you think you want to be doing. I also think that getting together with others who are experiencing the same desire to make transitions, as well as those who have successfully overcome such challenges, is invaluable. We realize we're not alone, can get help identifying and working through our blocks and share solutions or just empathize.

Lani: Are there books, CDs, DVDs or other resources that you would recommend to others going through transition?

Amy: No, none specifically, but I recommend finding trustworthy support persons who can keep up your spirits and cheer you on as you work toward a transition. I also recommend going into silence daily or weekly, through meditation or just being outdoors in nature to clear your mind and de-stress. Taking good care of oneself by eating, sleeping and exercising better really works magically, too, and making time to experience joy everyday.

Lani: Would you tell us more about your current intuitive guidance and healing work? How has what you've been through in your life led to finding your calling as an intuitive counselor?

Amy: I had been interested in "occult" things even as a child. Then, when I was 17 years old, my father suddenly died, and two things happened. First, I started having dreams where my father visited me. Second, my uncle suggested a book for me that had just been published: *Life After Life* by Raymond Moody, Jr., MD, PhD. Dr. Moody interviewed people who have had near-death experiences and then came back. He found patterns and similarities in what they encountered while they were clinically dead. This was very comforting to me, and I realized that there is much more to life than the material, physical plane that much of society considers the only "reality."

I followed my passion in the early 1990s by taking a variety of classes exploring metaphysical topics. My direct experience with the knowledge that the soul never dies – only the physical body dies – kept me going when my fiancé was diagnosed with cancer.

When I emailed my friends and colleagues with updates on my fiancé, I also shared my metaphysical beliefs to explain how I was feeling and coping. To my surprise, these messages were well-received and, in fact, most people were curious and open about it. Today, some of them they still regard me as a type of spiritual mentor, and they call on me when someone dies or has a health challenge or other type of life crisis. It's my privilege to share a metaphysical and "big picture" perspective with them to help them cope and heal.

After doing readings and healings for friends and family for eight or nine years, my teacher convinced me that I should offer my services to a wider audience. For over a dozen years, I've been helping people connect with a past life, a loved one who has "transitioned" out of their body or, keeping in mind that there's free will, the likely near-future and far-future consequences of their choices. It's been very rewarding to help others see beyond physics (metaphysics) and gain insight into their lives.

Lani: There are many ways of perceiving and experiencing reality. Thank you so much for sharing your gift with the readers of this book and with the world.

Seeing the glass half full as opposed to half empty allows for a more optimistic view of life. However, it is also important not to be too optimistic. Some people see the world through "rose-colored glasses" and are later devastated when traumatic life events intervene. It's vital to maintain a balanced and realistic yet, preferably, mostly upbeat approach to life. According to Dr. Martin E.P. Seligman's and colleagues' research in *Flourish: A Visionary New Understanding of Happiness and Well-being*:

> Optimists take action and have healthier lifestyles. Optimists believe that their actions matter, whereas pessimists believe they are helpless and nothing they do will matter. Optimists try, while pessimists lapse into passive helplessness. Optimists therefore act on medical advice readily, as George Vaillant found when the surgeon general's report on smoking and health came out in 1964; it was the optimists who gave up smoking, not the pessimists. Optimists take better care of themselves.[11]

So, in general, seeing the glass half full has an enormous impact, not only on how we view the world, but also on how we react and interact with it. Optimism can and does promote healthier choices, more options and a happier lifestyle… and, according to Seligman's earlier research in his *Learned Optimism: How to Change Your Mind and Your Life*, **optimism can be learned, even if a person is not optimistic by nature.**[12] In considering everything, events, other people and our own choices, the wisest course of action may be to see people and events as they are, then sort out the facts from opinion, keep your chin up and do your best to do your best. In other words, we don't have a choice about what events occur or how other people choose to behave, but we always have a choice about who we choose to be in relation to them.

We also have an option to drain that glass empty and refill it with the drink of our choice.

Glass Half Full and Empty Explorations:

If you have 5 to 10 minutes, answer the following:

In what way do you tend to view life? As a glass half empty or half full?

How is this way of seeing things impacting the range of choices and actions available to you?

What are some steps that you can take to practice being more optimistic and open to opportunities?

If you have more time, do the following:

Take a glass and fill it half-way with the drink of your choice. What does the liquid in the glass represent to you? For example, if it's water, is it life-giving? If it's wine, does that mean you value relaxation or the company of others? If it's cocoa, is there comfort in it? Drink that glass down and refill it with the drink of your choice and, if it feels good, say out loud: "I am choosing to live my life fully and with full acceptance of everything and everyone in it. I am choosing right now how I refill my glass and with what, where, how, why and with whom. I am the server of my own life."

Face your Demons.
Embrace Your Angels.

You can probably appreciate how your talents, your natural abilities, and your childhood dreams have added to your life and to the person you've become. But the traumatic events in your life—the experiences that left wounds within you—are an equally important part of the mix that will help you become all that you can be. Every insecurity, every fear, every tragedy, every obsession, broken relationship, and shameful incident holds clues that are leading you toward your most magnificent self.
–Debbie Ford, *The Secret of the Shadow: The Power of Owning Your Whole Story*

The Divided Selves

There's something we must recognize. We are often divided. We are not just isolated from one another, but we also segregate parts of ourselves, labeling these parts "bad" or "good," and project whatever we are not comfortable with onto others. This is not something we need to be ashamed of, beating ourselves up for what we learned or needed to do to survive. Rather, we can choose to be aware of, even if not fully comfortable with, all parts of ourselves to live more authentically. It is only when we become conscious that all aspects of the Self serve a function that we can make wiser choices based in awareness. We need to face our demons in order to embrace our angels.

An Interview with Gina Fedock-Robinson
Social Worker and Mom

A former client and friend of mine named Gina Fedock-Robinson had a transformative encounter with her shadow self, the dangerous and darker side of her nature. Over the course of several years, she experienced major life transitions, including graduation from college, working at her first full-time job, mourning several deaths in her family, moving from North Carolina to Michigan and, finally, fully accepting and embracing the fact that she was a lesbian and in love with a woman. Gina is beautiful, inside and out. She is 5'4" with dark, curly hair, fair skin and green eyes, and when we sat down to chat, she was working as a social worker with at-risk adult women who were pregnant. During our interview she told me that the Hindu goddess Kali best symbolized her struggles in facing her demons and embracing her angels during this transition to adulthood.

Kali, a Hindu goddess, represents death and destruction, and in myth she goes berserk in homicidal fervor on the battlefield, killing everyone in sight, demon and human, until her husband the Hindu god, Shiva, stops her by lying down under her feet. However, Kali is also a divine mother-goddess of creation and protection, cutting through illusion and allowing for freedom from fear of death.

Gina first encountered Kali when she was nineteen. She learned about this goddess in a feminist spirituality group, which explored ancient goddess cultures, honored the sacred feminine and helped her to discover all aspects of herself. "It was so much about changing my thoughts. I was in a sort of mental trap, relying on what I'd been raised with, rather than my own views," she explained. "I had always known that, for me, God was a Divine Mother. It's an interesting shift, as I was raised and surrounded by God the Father."

I asked Gina how this reconciled with the Judeo-Christian upbringing in her youth, and she replied, "I grew up with this idea of Jesus as Savior, but Kali allowed for a female model of saving oneself: for liberation, permission, picking up that knife and discerning what needs to go and what stays." Gina's family of origin had instilled in her a system of belief that did not align with who she really was. Gina realized with her transition into adulthood that it was a matter of being true to herself versus living a lie or even someone else's truth. She finished answering this question by adding, "I had to figure out how to integrate my own world view and values."

However, Gina is also aware of the danger inherent in the unacknowledged or untamed shadow self. Kali is depicted in many Tantric and Hindu sources as having four arms, carrying a sword or trident and a severed head in two of the hands, while the other two hands are often shown in *mudras* or blessing postures. She is portrayed with black or blue skin, red eyes, covered in blood, with her tongue protruding, while wearing a necklace of skulls and a girdle of human arms. According to David Gordon White's *Tantra in Practice*, Kali is "often depicted naked which symbolizes her being beyond the covering of Maya [illusion].... She has no permanent qualities—she will continue to exist when the universe ends. It is therefore believed that the concepts of color, light, good, bad do not apply to her—she is the pure, un-manifested energy, the Adi-shakti."[13] Thus, Kali is primal, a life-death force. She is, like many gods and goddesses in ancient civilizations, a divine expression of the wholeness of creation-destruction. She is not immoral or even amoral; she is beyond human comprehension.

While Kali allows for creation, she is also wisely feared and respected as a destructive force. "I think, for me, not falling in love with destruction is important," Gina said, nodding thoughtfully. "With Kali it's about something eternal. In some ways she embodies the whole attitude that power comes back effortlessly, without thinking about it or looking back. It's the courage to simply be." Gina concluded, "Kali is also primal anger. That was something that I wasn't able to express earlier. It was such strong confirmation to trust that in strong emotions, like anger, there's truth. It's about owning it, knowing oneself, and being ready to lose whatever may be lost." Being authentic means being honest with oneself and others, even if it means that others won't agree with you and may judge you. As Gina shared with me later, "I've been thinking more and more about how being honest in the present moment is the goal—I then am truth—not perfection, because being true is the goal." Being whole is about awareness, integrity and self-acceptance.

My Survivor's Story

Over the past twenty-five years, I have discovered parts of myself that have lain dormant for a very long time. In counseling and meditation I have become aware of the survivor parts of myself that are not pleasant to encounter or even admit. I call these darker aspects of myself my "vampire" and my "siren" selves. Yet, these shadow parts of myself have helped me to survive some of the greatest trials in my life. When I am aware of their allure and the danger of falling into addiction, I can usually break the cycle of destruction and use their power for creation instead.

Everyone is familiar with the vampire, an undead temptress made popular in movies and books, who must drink the life blood of her victims in order to survive, who disintegrates in the light of day or can be destroyed with a wooden stake through the heart. For those of you unfamiliar with the siren, this creature is often confused with the mermaid. In Greco-Roman mythology sirens were part woman and part bird and would lure sailors to their deaths along rocky coasts at sea.

Sometimes the sirens' seductive singing made men forget to work, eat or drink, and they would die pining for what could never be. Both of these creatures are predators, as well as prey. They are unable to survive without causing destruction but, inevitably, their prey hunt them down, and their own insatiable desires are what actually destroy them.

As a survivor of sexual assault in my childhood, I learned early on that the world is not a safe place. A married couple whom my parents trusted were predators, who used the bait of their foster daughter to lure unsuspecting victims like myself into what seemed like an innocent "sleepover," but was instead a trap to molest children. I was drugged and made to feel I had imagined or dreamed the whole experience, but I was also told to say nothing, that no one would believe me anyway, confusing and contradictory messages. I repressed the memory for over two decades out of fear, shame and guilt. It was an experience so horrific, I didn't even know the words to describe what had happened to me…until college.

I came into my sexuality later than most American women. I was nineteen when I was with my first lover. This experience of pleasure and pain triggered in me something intoxicating and addictive. I felt flooded with power while, at the same time, desperation. "Love" was the only way a respectable young woman in the nineties could legitimize her sexual urges, so I fell in love, hard and often. I lived a double life, honors student by day and wild woman on the weekends, drinking too much at clubs and selecting several unsuitable partners, men who had their own addictions and who were incapable of real love.

The Shadow Selves that Save Me

My demons had me in their grip, until I realized that these demons were actually the disconnected parts of myself, the vampire and the siren, trying to get my attention. It was me who was the hunter and the temptress, "in control," or so I thought. Yet, I had been the victim and survivor, caught in someone else's web, and finding myself ensnared over and over. I did not yet love myself, so I chose empty relationships as a way to remain "independent" and "empowered," when actually these affairs left me co-dependent and disempowered. I would not allow myself to love and be loved, out of a semi-conscious fear that I was unlovable, so I chose men who could not love me, much less love themselves. It was only after several very bad relationships and crises and graduation from college that I realized I wanted to turn my life around. I wanted to love and be loved in return.

I had always cared about people. Strangers would share with me their most private and painful secrets, sensing that I cared. I wanted a life of meaningful work and service. I had fought against acknowledging my vampire and siren selves for so long, trying to be a "good girl," without acknowledging these shadow sides of myself, who took over whenever given half a chance. I had to be careful of the triggers, drinking too much alcohol and being on my own at dance clubs, that allowed my shadow aspects to take control. I had to remain sober, avoid going to nightclubs alone and find healthier ways to cope with the pain, anger and fear. It took over a year of counseling in graduate school and volunteer service with the Boulder County Rape Crisis Team to bring them back into my consciousness and to address the core issue of being victimized in childhood.

Then ten years later, when I was a hotline counselor in Ann Arbor, where I supported survivors of sexual assault and domestic violence, I also needed counseling for what the training and hotline calls triggered within me. I learned in training that many survivors of sexual assault or domestic violence take the blame onto themselves as a way of regaining a false sense of control over what was stolen from them. I learned that some victims become predators as a way to cope. In my twenties I had sought to ensnare men at the nightclubs with my sexual power, but I ended up being caught in my own web, feeling emptied and wasted. I recognized my pattern of self-abuse was a reflection of the early abuse, and that my vampire and siren selves were actually there to show me when I was starting to teeter, out of balance. If I could acknowledge their existence and listen to them, they would tell me when I needed to reach out for help and support. When I reached out to a professional counselor and a couple of close friends, I found a frightened, cornered child inside, who needed to understand fully that what had happened in my childhood was not my fault and that I could take responsibility for my life as an adult and heal these wounds.

Still later, as a teacher and a rape and domestic violence hotline crisis counselor, and finally as a transitions life coach, I found I could use my experiences—all of my experiences—to create work that might benefit others, as well as myself. I had developed several tools and strategies for self-care and balance. These served me and could serve others, who were ready to take the courageous and transformative leap of faith in their own lives. I was also grateful to be a writer, as writing was a mode of expression through which I could lay my demons out on the page and watch as they transformed by the light of day into something different: lighter and freer than before.

My siren, the seductive singer, could become the Divine voice, expressing my deepest hopes. My vampire, the bloodthirsty temptress, could transform into a healer. Both would tell me when I needed to fulfill my needs in other ways, through rest, nutrition, exercise, loving interconnections and meditation. My darker aspects were actually there to protect me, if I didn't let them take over. If I could reach out for support and acknowledge the damage they represented, then I could embrace these newfound angels. I could heal and transform them and myself.

I want to make it understood that addictions are still always present for me, just in greater or lesser degree. They take different forms at different times: food, shopping, caffeine, alcohol, men. I still "fall off the wagon" from time to time, and it is still deeply painful and embarrassing whenever that happens. However, when I mindfully replace something unhealthy with something healthy and have compassion for myself and others anyway—even when I fail—I find I can cope better than when hiding in shame or blame. I can more swiftly return to balance, instead of teetering between extremes, when I allow myself to admit I am in trouble and need some help. When I allow myself to be vulnerable, ironically I become most strong and in touch with all of who I am.

According to Brené Brown in her groundbreaking book *Daring Greatly: How the Courage to Be Vulnerable Transforms the Way We Live, Love, Parent and Lead*:

> Our rejection of vulnerability often stems from our associating it with dark emotions like fear, shame, grief, sadness, and disappointment—emotions that we don't want to discuss, even when they profoundly affect the way we live, love, work, and even lead. What most of us fail to understand and what took me a decade of research to learn is that vulnerability is also the cradle of the emotions and experiences that we crave. Vulnerability is the birthplace of love, belonging, joy, courage, empathy, and creativity. It is the source of hope, empathy, accountability, and authenticity. If we want greater clarity in our purpose or deeper and more meaningful spiritual lives, vulnerability is the path.[14]

While writing about these encounters with my shadow selves in the past and present, I am reminded that it is only when we accept our dark sides that we are aware enough to choose the light. We can't just turn off certain emotions because we don't want to feel them. If we do, we lose access to other emotions. Brené Brown's research over the past decade has shown that it is through vulnerability that we discover other aspects of who we are. We all have something we must face, deal with and overcome. Even when we face our demons, there are times when some may still return to bite us on the ass. However, they have much more power when we are in denial, shame and fear. We gain wisdom and freedom when we can accept, empathize and love all parts of ourselves while in a state of vulnerability. This is not to be confused with weakness or giving up. When we love all aspects of ourselves, there is compassion for ourselves and for others. When we face our demons, we can finally recognize and embrace our angels, too.

We need not do this alone. There are several resources available to support our exploration of Self and growth into wholeness, including therapy and counseling, religious or spiritual affiliations, books, CDs and DVDs, organizations and programs devoted to healing and, last but never least, the love and concern of close friends and family. There are two books that I highly recommend to clients and friends recovering from trauma, who would like to use writing as a tool to heal. Louise DeSalvo's *Writing as a Way of Healing: How Telling Our Stories Transforms Our Lives* is based on over twenty years of research into writing as a healing process and includes insightful exercises and poignant stories based on other writers' lives, such as Audre Lorde, Henry Miller, Virginia Woolf and Isabel Allende, who have used their own writing to heal themselves.[15] The other book, *Writing to Change the World* by Mary Pipher, encourages us to bring our power as writers to the larger world.[16] In this book Pipher combines practical guidelines and exercises, as well as uplifting stories of writing that have made a positive and lasting difference in the world. Both books came to me at pivotal moments in my healing, and both have allowed me to support others going through recovery.

Knowing that all parts of the Self serve a valuable function, we can integrate our separate selves and choose to be whole. Integrating light and dark parts, as well as the full spectrum of color, allows us the insight, courage and wisdom to reconcile the past, lovingly accept whomever we are now and imagine and create whomever we want to become in the future.

Face your Demons, Embrace Your Angels Explorations:

If you have 5 to 10 minutes, answer the following:

Are there parts of yourself that you're ashamed of or you have hidden out of fear? What are they?

What were the experiences in your life that have led to your feeling ashamed or needing to hide these parts?

What would you tell your best friend if they had a similar experience happen in their lives?

Chances are you would comfort that friend. Can you do that for yourself? Can you seek out sources of support, a counselor, therapist, minister or trusted friend or family member, who can help you face your demons and embrace your angels? Who or what are these sources of support?

Is there something in the experience that brought you insight or knowledge about that disconnected part of yourself? If so, what?

Can you release the pain and suffering around that experience, yet retain the love and lessons that came out of it?

How can you transform a "demon" into an "angel"? What are the emotions of fear, shame and/or anxiety protecting you from? How can they become your allies?

If you have more time, answer the following:

Go to the library or online to research and discover more about Kali, Pele or other creation/destruction Gods and Goddesses, or to learn more about vampires, sirens or other shadows in folklore. See what parts of the Shadow Self you most relate to and why. Record your reflections in a journal or collage. Reach out for sources of support, a counselor, therapist or close friends, if needed, as this work may unexpectedly bring up painful memories or feelings.

Leaving Baggage Behind

Each of us has the right and the responsibility to assess the road which lies ahead and those over which we have traveled, and if the future road looms ominous or unpromising, and the road back uninviting, then we need to gather our resolve and carrying only the necessary baggage, step off that road into another direction. If the new choice is also unpalatable, without embarrassment, we must be ready to change that one as well.
–Maya Angelou

Literal and Figurative Baggage

I saw His Holiness the Dalai Lama in Ann Arbor on April 19th and 20th, 2008, when he came to speak about *Engaging Wisdom and Compassion* at the University of Michigan's Crisler Arena. It was an odd choice of venues, with stadium seating used primarily for sports events and rock concerts.

It was chilly for mid-April in Michigan, so I dressed in capris and Skechers, with a long sleeve shirt and sweater. My partner, Justin, had plans to visit his ailing father that day, and he kindly dropped me off a block from the arena, aware that the parking was limited. There were also protests going on. About a hundred Chinese people called the Dalai Lama a "terrorist" and "criminal" because of the Tibetan protests that had just taken place in his native country. Ironically, they were shouting, "No Olympics!"—even though I'm certain they meant to chant "yes" to the upcoming Beijing-hosted games and "no" to the Dalai Lama's talk and got it confused in the translation.

Because of the Dalai Lama's controversial political status,

security was not allowing bags or purses of any kind into the arena. Unfortunately, I was not aware of this added security measure and had brought along a shoulder bag the size of a Bible with several compartments to organize my life. Now, I should tell you that this bag held additional "weight" for me besides just the contents. I had bought it several months before on sale at Macy's for $85 (marked down from $120) without Justin's knowledge. I had felt guilty about the purchase, because I had gone beyond our budget, and so I had hidden it from him until I came clean a week later. In addition I had bought it for my 20th high school reunion the previous year. I had bought it because it was beautiful and practical with leather patches of varying hues stitched together, so that I could use it with several different outfits, but it was also a Lucky brand bag and a status symbol. In short, it was a crutch to help me feel better about myself going back to Honolulu for my 20th high school reunion. It was a bag that proclaimed, "Wow! She's got great taste…and money…and a heck of a lot of emotional baggage to sort through!"

I was aware of these thoughts, as I waited in line wondering what I should do. I could call Justin's cell phone and ask him to come back for the purse? But he was already running late, and I didn't want to inconvenience him further. I could try to smuggle it in? A ridiculous thought quickly dismissed, when I considered I'd look six months pregnant with a lumpy baby, and the security guard, who was just trying to do his job, was standing there right in front of me. Or I could leave it behind? But there were no lockers and no way to ensure it would be there when I returned. With barely a moment's hesitation, I pulled out the essentials: my wallet, planner, cell phone and keys, and left the purse, containing hand cream, lipstick and coupons, behind on the ground near the entrance. It looked deflated, a little depressed, as if I had let it down, but I left it behind on the ground nonetheless. As I entered the arena to hear the spiritual teachings of an enlightened leader, I felt lighter, with only a trace of regret at choosing to leave my literal and figurative baggage behind.

While I am not a Buddhist, I do find a great deal of value in some Buddhist texts and teachings. The lecture was delivered in the Dalai Lama's native Tibetan tongue and translated into English. It was about the awakening of *bodhisattvas* into buddhas, beings who choose to be in service to humankind, even though they have attained enlightenment and could leave the Earth behind. The Dalai Lama described how, as we awaken, we will naturally release individual grasping and suffering and ultimately serve for the good of all. A couple of hours later, when I went outside for lunch, the purse was gone and, with it, my guilt and shame about materialism. I realized that the baggage was not so much about purchasing a purse but, rather, the way in which I had done it, sneaking it and feeling guilty because of it, as well as the reason for buying it, to feel good about myself, because I didn't already feel inherently worthy. I left with a stronger sense of purpose and a new way of viewing my role in the world, a renewed commitment to practice meditation and make wiser, conscious and more loving choices.

Other Kinds of "Baggage"

More recently, I have been thinking about other emotional baggage I have carried for far too long, all related to the illusory feeling of unworthiness. A college friend of mine posted a song dedication to me on Facebook that struck an unexpected raw nerve inside me: "Bad Girl" by Madonna. In the video a striking *femme fatale*, played by Madonna, is shown murdered, with the police on the scene to investigate, and then we see a film noir-type narrative in which she is being watched by what seems like a stalker, played by Christopher Walken, until we realize through the course of the video that he is not her killer, but instead the Angel of Death. I was speechless as I watched these scenes unfold and felt a mixture of emotions so powerful, rage, pain and terror, which short-circuited me, and I went completely numb for about a day.

As a survivor of childhood sexual assault, I had found a variety of ways to cope. Some were functional, like staying in my head and thinking too much or going numb whenever my feelings overwhelmed me and were too painful to bear, and others were dysfunctional, like trying to take back my sexual power as a college-aged woman by drinking vodka straight and picking up men in dance clubs. At the end of the video, Madonna's killer is a young man whom she picks up at a bar.

There is no way my college friend could have known about my past—as I was so good at hiding it, even from myself—and I should also note here that he had posted that video in reply to a playful "poke" of a post I had put up for him, "Material Girl," meant to tease him about his champagne tastes but Prosecco budget (which, based on the story above, you can certainly see I relate to). At first I was so traumatized, my natural defense mechanism humor kicked in, and I even jokingly replied to his post, writing "Spot on, darling…but I'm doing better these days," which of course couldn't have been further from the truth.

That evening, as the iceberg in my heart started to melt, rupture and fall apart, I found myself sobbing into my towel at the Honolulu Club and thinking to myself, "I thought I was over this shit!" (Definition of Shit? Trauma. False beliefs about my Self. Thinking myself worthless, when in actuality each of us is precious and unique and irreplaceable.) Clearly, all those years of therapy, meditation and supposed self-awareness had led to this…yet another layer to dissolve, another emotional bag to unpack.

I wrote to him that evening and demanded an apology, which he immediately provided and, deeply contrite, he also added two new Madonna songs to my wall, "Cherish" and "Sorry." I realized, then, that I had overreacted and accused someone I care a great deal about of being incredibly cruel. I felt the blood rise to my cheeks, a fist in my gut. I was horrified that I had almost de-friended him. I felt he deserved a better explanation, so I sent him the link to my earlier blog posting: "Face Your Demons; Embrace Your Angels" and apologized.

We exchanged several more songs and e-mails, and I spiraled out of control for another week or so, oscillating wildly, like a Coke bottle violently shaken, ready to explode. It took a long time to land on my feet again. During that time I told my two best friends what had happened when I overreacted. Saying it out loud made the experience less scary, less overwhelming, more understandable, a normal reaction to trauma and one I could get past, yet again. Of course, I gave them edited versions, especially my partner, because I did not wish to inflict pain upon him. Given the circumstances and who I am, I told myself I wanted to shield him from it...that would be the noble part of me. The other part of me wanted to *die*, and being an English major, I meant it in the Shakespearean sense (look it up, if you must) and literally, too.

I had to find a way to put those bags away: take them out of the proverbial closet...maybe move them to the garage, throw them away or pile them on a bonfire and get rid of them for good? I realized then that the *femme fatale* in the Madonna video is herself the killer. She chooses her own method of self-destruction. By choosing actions based on repressed suffering, she mindlessly repeats over and over again her own abuse, in order to heal a wound that can't be healed without fully feeling it, processing it and letting it go. Thus, she hurts herself and those around her over and over again. I understood that it was me who was breaking my own heart, and, thus, I could choose to stop it.

It took a lot of time and a lot of soul searching—and a lot of writing and music and real love—before I could integrate these feelings, ideals and beliefs about who I thought I was versus who I am and, most importantly, who I would choose to become.

What You Can Do to Lighten Your Load

If you are also unpacking emotional baggage, here's some advice from someone who has been to hell and back several times.

1) I recommend finding trustworthy, loving and reliable support persons who care about you and who will listen without judgment. These "touchstone people," as I call them, can be professional counselors, friends, mentors or others, but what they have in common is that they will keep things in perspective as you work toward transition and transformation.
2) I also recommend going into silence daily, through meditation or being outdoors in nature to clear your mind. Often the answers are deep inside of us, if we would just stop and listen.
3) Taking good care of yourself by eating, sleeping and exercising as needed.

Finally, whenever I'm in doubt about the right course of action to take, I ask myself three important questions:

1) What is my intention?
2) Am I thinking about the past or future, or am I living fully in this moment?

3) What action would be best for the highest good of all concerned, including myself?

With those three questions it is no longer about others or just me alone. With those questions I will always reach higher ground.

Leaving Behind Baggage Exploration:

If you have 5 to 10 minutes, answer the following:

Do you have any symbolic "baggage" that you need or want to leave behind? What type of baggage is it? Designer? Canvas? Sequined? Patent leather? Vegan? Is it shoulder slung across the body or a briefcase or a clutch or something else? Each of these choices offers a clue to the kind of baggage you are carrying.
    For example the following could mean:

Designer: You care about what others think of you.

Canvas: You're down-to-earth but may need more sparkle in your life.

Sequined: You need to feel more beautiful and attractive, not just showing off the outside, Diva!

Patent leather: Are you trying to fit in or needing to burst out?

Vegan: You just need to stop trying to be Jesus or the Buddha or a saint and just be yourself.

Shoulder slung: You like to keep your hands free, now free your mind.

Briefcase: You are all work and no play. This will make you very unhappy.

Clutch: You hold tightly to what you think you want. Why not switch to a wristlet so you can let loose once in a while?

You get the idea…everything we wear, decorate our lives with and the partners we choose indicate who we think we are or should be. I invite you to consider what you could do with a different choice.

If you have more time, answer the following:

Unpack your baggage, literally and figuratively: Make a list on a sheet of self-adhesive stickers of all the resentments, regrets, pain and failures you have had in your life. Place these labels on rocks or bricks. Pack these in a sturdy suitcase and carry this suitcase with you for a period of time, an hour or more.

Notice how you really want to put this baggage down after only a short time? Imagine having to carry it the rest of your life. You've already carried it in your heart for a number of years. Are you ready to release burdens from the past that no longer serve you? Are you ready to forgive yourself and others?

If so, unpack the "baggage" and re-label each stone or brick with specific insights that you learned from that difficult experience. (For example, with *shame* you can now label that transformed feeling compassion, because you have learned how to heal the hurt in yourself and understand the suffering of others.) Notice that even our past pain can yield perspective, compassion and wisdom.

Checking In

Dear Readers,

Now that we are midway through the book, if you have chosen not to do the explorations, ask yourself why?

What is holding you back from examining these memories and experiences?

What and who could help you to do so?

You are also always welcome to go on to the next section and come back to any exploration you were not yet ready to complete. This is your book to use as you desire.

Me ke aloha, (with love)
Lani

Emotional Balance, Mindful Movement and Relaxation©:

This self-exploration offers a quick and easy way to evaluate your emotions, how you may habitually express them and how to bring them into better balance. ~20-30 minutes

1. What are some emotions that we, in this culture, typically consider to be opposites (e.g. happy/sad)? List several others here:

2. Consider that there may *not* be opposites in emotions, rather, that feelings may exist in a balanced state or in extreme states of too much or too little:

Emotional balance and the two dysfunctional extremes

+ extreme (too much)	Balanced	- extreme (too little)
Rage/Hatred	Anger	Apathy/Numbness
Envy	Jealousy	Apathy/Numbness
Terror	Fear	Apathy/Numbness
Despair	Sadness/Sorrow	Apathy/Numbness
Obsession	Love	Apathy/Numbness
Forced Cheer	Happiness	Apathy/Numbness
Blind Faith	Hope	Apathy/Numbness

When looking at this chart, we can clearly see that even feelings that are often thought of as "positive" or "good," like love, happiness and hope, can be dysfunctional and damaging to the self or to others when taken to either extreme. They can transform into obsession, forced cheer or blind faith, on the one hand, or apathy and numbness, on the other. Feelings typically described as "negative" or "bad"—anger, jealousy, fear and sadness or sorrow—are actually appropriate responses to a given set of circumstances. Taken to either extreme, however, they become rage or hatred, envy, terror and despair or apathy and numbness. Each extreme either represents too much, an over-expression, or too little, a suppression, of balanced human emotion. Each extreme has dangerous consequences for the well-being of the individual and often for others.

Rather than setting up emotions in commonly understood oppositions to one another—good/bad, happiness/sorrow, hope/despair—this three-part approach more clearly illustrates how feelings can interrelate and affect one another by their over-expression or suppression. Over time, people who cannot feel fear or anger, for example, may also begin to no longer feel happiness or other feelings. Hence, we see the eventual state of apathy and numbness for all suppressed emotions.

In Eastern thought mindfulness allows for the insight and non-judgment of all emotions, thoughts and physical sensations. What this entails is awareness without acting habitually from the negative emotive, thought or physical states or even having attachments to the positive ones. This balanced three-part model of emotion helps us see that all emotions have value and function, even the negative ones like anger or jealousy, and that over-valuing the positive ones, even love, can be harmful. Trying to be happy, hopeful or loving all the time is simply not possible, nor is trying to avoid anger, jealousy, fear or sorrow. We, as human beings, are meant to feel and express a full range of feelings, not just the "good" ones. When we deny, hide or try to destroy emotions within ourselves, we also lose the ability to understand them in others.

3. Study the three-part balance of emotions and the two dysfunctional extremes chart below. Assess where you believe you are *right now* on the continuum in terms of your balance of emotion, and place a check mark there.

Emotional balance and the two dysfunctional extremes

+ extreme (too much)	Balanced	- extreme (too little)
Rage/Hatred	Anger	Apathy/Numbness
Envy	Jealousy	Apathy/Numbness
Terror	Fear	Apathy/Numbness
Despair	Sadness/Sorrow	Apathy/Numbness
Obsession	Love	Apathy/Numbness
Forced Cheer	Happiness	Apathy/Numbness
Blind Faith	Hope	Apathy/Numbness

4. Which emotion(s) cause you the most discomfort?

Which one(s) seem to come out when you least expect them to and in ways that make you or others feel uncomfortable?

Which one(s) is/are the most difficult to show yourself or other people?

5. Why, when and how did expressing these emotions in a balanced way become challenging for you? Consider past events, family and friends, mentors and foes, and faulty beliefs and misperceptions of self as potential causes. List them here for each challenging emotion:

Habitual emotion(s):   Why/When/How an
                       imbalance occurred:

6. Now let's brainstorm ways to bring each emotional imbalance back into balanced expression. Remember all emotions are normal and serve a purpose, even the ones we might consider "bad." Consider ways you can begin to express your feelings in a more balanced, healthier way that will cause no harm to yourself or others. Be as specific as possible:

Habitual emotion(s):   Way(s) I can express it/them
                       in better balance:

Our Interconnected World

Meaningful Work

In order to feel like a somebody, we do not need fame or celebrity. For most of us, there is reward enough if we contribute something of ourselves to others, and have that contribution duly recognized.
–Robert W. Fuller, *Somebodies and Nobodies: Overcoming the Abuse of Rank*

Work: a Job, a Vocation or a Calling?

In challenging economic times, most of us are grateful to have a job, any job, but we serve ourselves and others best when we are doing work that is meaningful. For some folks it's the satisfaction found in a job well done, the ability to pay bills and support their families. Other people find meaning in a vocation or calling that transcends basic physical or emotional needs, inspiring them to reach new heights, challenging themselves and improving the lives of others. However, we can make any type of work worthwhile when we focus on how, why and where we can best use our abilities.

One of the most effective ways to know if your work is currently meaningful is to ask yourself this simple question: "Do I look forward to going to work each day?" If you can't honestly answer, "Yes!" then it's time to reflect, assess and take action. It may be that most days go well and that there are just a few moments of frustration. Or it may be that you really wanted to do something else and got caught up in someone else's expectations or dreams for you. Maybe you started out loving what you do and are bored now, needing a change of pace? In any case, even the most mundane or menial jobs can be made worthwhile, if we approach them with a sense of service, creating significant experiences and relationships. As Dr. Martin Luther King, Jr. wrote, "If it falls to your lot to be a street sweeper, sweep streets like Michelangelo painted pictures, like Shakespeare wrote poetry, like Beethoven composed music; sweep streets so well that all the hosts of heaven and earth will have to pause and say, 'Here lived a great street sweeper, who swept his job well.'" We can choose to shift our perspective, take pride in our work, no matter what it is, and make any job rewarding.

Career Changes and How to Make Any Job Meaningful

Career change is one of the life transitions my clients find most difficult, due to the loss of a sense of security and income, as well as fears and self-identification with the work they do. Our language supports this job self-identification, as we say things like, "I am a teacher" and not "I do teaching." It is important to be aware of this preconceived notion and how it impacts each of us. Our culture values certain fields of work, while devaluing others, not just in terms of status or money, but also in the undervaluing of the people who do it. It is crucial to find worth in what we do and not "buy into" (even our language supports the concept of monetary value over other kinds of worth) cultural biases towards certain kinds of work.

Many of my clients have found themselves laid off in this difficult economy and have had to scramble to find a new job before their unemployment benefits ran out. Flexibility and optimism are vital in any job search, but especially so when a job loss was not a result of one's own choice. One coaching client confided in me that, after seventeen moves and a handful of unsatisfying, entry-level jobs over the past couple of years, he was "just trying to survive." He was certain that his feelings of resentment came across to his co-workers and boss.

We discussed his fears and concerns and uncovered a false "master assessment" that was unconsciously affecting his work life. A "master assessment," in Newfield Network coaching terminology, is a belief, often untrue, that controls you and seems to be real.[17] His subconscious master assessment was: "Sometimes you have to do what you don't want to do in order to survive."

We talked about where this belief had come from (his family in a sincere effort to prepare him for the "real world") and what had reinforced it over the years (working at jobs he hated just to pay bills) and how this formed a vicious circle of taking unfulfilling jobs he didn't want because they provided for his basic needs. While there were real-life and practical reasons this belief had served him the past, it was now holding him back from taking more risks and pursuing work that was more in alignment with his true calling.

I asked him how he could modify the language of this unhelpful belief so that it could offer more flexibility and potential for change in the future. We wrestled with the language for a while: "Sometimes it's necessary to do what you don't want to do in order to survive, but survival is not all there is to life;" "It is important to do what I want in order to survive and thrive." Finally, he came up with the answer on his own: "All the work that I do is in service to my greater vision."

A week later, he reported that, by repeating this phrase silently whenever frustrated with his jobs, his perspective on his work had shifted, even though the actual work was exactly the same. He no longer saw it as giving up his time for someone else. He became more enthusiastic, and his boss noticed and offered him a full-time position.

Language is powerful. Words create our realities. It is

important to consider what you may have been telling yourself all these years and whether or not it serves you anymore.

Another way to shift your perspective in a job that has become unsatisfying is to create consistent significant experiences while at work. How often do you feel challenged or interested in the work you do? If work has become boring or routine, it may be worthwhile to ask your boss for a challenging assignment or to take a course or some additional training that could help make your work fresh again.

Another way to create meaning is simply to shift your perception of the value of the work you do. Can you see how your work impacts other people and the larger world? Do you perceive how your work is important? Is there a deeper meaning and significance that you can create in your day-to-day schedule?

The Power of Positive Psychology

According to Dr. Martin E.P. Seligman in his groundbreaking work on well-being and positive psychology, *Flourish: A Visionary New Understanding of Happiness and Well-Being*:

> We think too much about what goes wrong and not enough about what goes right in our lives. Of course, sometimes it makes sense to analyze bad events so that we can learn from them and avoid them in the future. However, people tend to spend more time thinking about what is bad in life than is helpful.[18]

He recommends an easy-to-do exercise called "What Went Well" or "Three Blessings," which will help people practice positive thinking and well-being awareness. This can be applied toward life in general, as well as regarding work-specific issues. Every evening, set aside some time and write down three things that went well. It can be done on the computer or in a journal, but it's important to have a record that you can refer back to. These three things do not need to be of major importance but could include anything that went well, such as "I am getting along with my colleagues," "My boss appreciates my work" or "New office supplies came in today." Then, once you have your list of three things, answer: "Why did this happen?" next to it. Using the examples above: "Because I'm making an effort to be more friendly," "My boss is a caring person" and "The office manager is good at his/her job." Dr. Seligman asserts that this simple exercise has been shown to decrease depression and increase happiness. It is very important to note how often what went well was due to external factors and other people versus our own self-direction and choices that allow us the freedom to create opportunities in our own lives.

Cultivate Advisors, Mentors and Sponsors

It is also possible to foster worthwhile relationships at work with mentors and other people who are supporters of the work you do. Carla A. Harris, award-winning Managing Director at Morgan Stanley, motivational speaker and author of *Expect to Win: 10 Proven Strategies for Thriving in the Workplace*, suggests creating three key relationships in the workplace: the advisor, the mentor and the sponsor. She defines each of these as people within your field who will be supportive of your career goals, but she describes each role slightly differently.

According to Harris, an advisor is "someone who can answer your discrete career questions, those that may be isolated questions pertaining to your career but are not necessarily in context of your broader career goals."[19] In other words, a variety of people can fill this role. These will be people who have experience or information that would be helpful to you in general, but you would not trust them with specific questions regarding your career strategy.

A mentor is "someone who can answer your discrete career questions *and* who can give you specific tailored career advice. You can tell them 'the good, the bad, and the ugly' about your career, and you can trust their feedback will be helpful to your career progression."[20] A mentor is someone you trust to share the ins and outs and specific details of your career plan and whom you are confident has your best interests at heart. Sometimes an advisor may become a mentor over time.

And, finally, a sponsor is defined by Harris as "someone who will use their internal political social capital to move your career forward within an organization."[21] Most people only think of the first two types of relationships, in which you can trust a more experienced colleague for advice, insight and strategies into how a organization functions, but they don't realize how important a sponsor is in "closed door" meetings in which decisions regarding your progress are made.

Carla Harris advises cultivating a diverse group of people in terms of seniority, ethnicity, gender and professional background to gain the most benefit in all of these relationships. These will be people whom you admire and respect and who should not have conflicts of interest in advising, supporting or standing up for you. She points out that it is important to offer mutually beneficial support to your advisors, mentors and sponsors by being a person with integrity whom they will be proud to work with, and by offering helpful, viable information in return. However, she also points out that consulting with "non-fans" can be helpful in understanding what others perceive to be your weaknesses in the office. By acknowledging and acting on this seemingly negative feedback in an objective and proactive way, you can then redirect office perceptions by selecting three adjectives, such as tough, fair and competent, to consistently embody in the position or field of work to which you aspire. Thus, it is possible—even in extremely competitive fields such as investment banking in which Harris works—to build informative, supportive and mutually beneficial relationships at work.

Another angle to consider in seeking meaningful work is that it is an opportunity for growth. While many people fear change and dread searching for a new job, a job search itself can be meaningful, inspiring and life-changing. I've seen many clients explore and express aspects of themselves they had never before had time to develop. Hobbies, volunteer work or other interests can sometimes become the foundation for a new career.

Being away from the full-time working world while raising children can be an opportunity to pursue part-time work in another field or to do volunteer work that expands one's skills and maintains and even enhances social networks. New training and educational opportunities in a different field can expand your horizons, and there are numerous opportunities for creating meaning through your work. The key is to follow your passions, stay connected with those who can help you (and whom you can help) in the future and to be flexible and keep your skill sets strong and varied in order to meet the changing needs of future employers. Or, if you are courageous and perseverant, you may decide to start that new business venture.

In any case, things happen, other people are who they are, but we still get to choose how we react and act in any work situation. We can make many types of work situations meaningful by learning from them, being aware of our false master beliefs, creating meaningful experiences and positive interactions with others and moving forward with an appreciation of all of our experiences.

An Interview with Dr. Arash Babaoff Pediatrician at the Cincinnati Children's Hospital Emergency Department and Volunteer with Operation Smile

http://www.operationsmile.org/index.html

I have known Dr. Arash Babaoff for over two decades. Arash's parents are first generation Iranian-American, and he grew up in Iran, Switzerland and, later, the suburbs of Michigan. When I was considering whom to interview for this book, he immediately came to mind as a role model of someone who has overcome adversity and self-doubt in order to fulfill his calling through meaningful work and service. He has gone beyond the scope of work in a hospital emergency room. He travels all over the world as a volunteer with medical teams who perform life-altering surgeries on children with cleft lips and palates. He wanted me to be certain to emphasize that he does not perform these surgeries himself but is part of the support team, not wanting to divert attention away from the surgeons who do this meaningful work. This is just one example of Arash's integrity and humility. He inspires me in my own work to find ways to reach out to others that will have lasting impact. I had the chance to interview him via e-mail in February 2013.

Lani: Many people are seeking meaningful interaction and a sense of purpose in their work. What led you to do the meaningful work you do?

Arash: I have found that my meaningful interactions are steeped in intimacy. On a personal level, I find that I am fed by that intimacy and give compassion in return. The nature of my work in medicine lends itself easily to both intimacy and compassion. I know I am in the right place.

Lani: How did you find your calling in medicine? What led you to work with children at Cincinnati Children's Hospital?

Arash: Though my parents have both been in the medical field, I didn't come to the realization that medicine was my calling until the very end of college. It was a tortuous path, but a friend's courage in the face of ovarian cancer prompted me to pursue medicine. For me, the path has taken both time and maturity and continues to reveal itself.

I started working at summer camps for children during college. The bonds that I forged with those young people solidified my resolve to always work with children. Caring for children and adolescents felt very natural to me and, in turn, I felt I received unconditionally from them. Once I was in the clinical years of medical school, it became obvious quite quickly that whatever rotation I was doing, I enjoyed it much more fully when young people were the focus.

I had mentors in pediatrics who were both friends and inspirations. One particular mentor who practiced pediatric oncology was particularly influential in guiding me to the pediatric residency program in Cincinnati, for which I will always be grateful. I have been able to design my schedule at the hospital in a way that allows me to continue my volunteer efforts. Also, to this day, I continue to be "the camp doctor" during the summers.

Lani: How did you first find out about Operation Smile, and what encouraged you to volunteer your free time to become a part of the teams that perform facial cleft surgeries around the world?

Arash: I had known about Operation Smile when I was a pediatric resident but had the opportunity to become involved after the events of 9/11/2001, when people were more afraid of going abroad. Operation Smile was in need of physicians to go on a mission to Nairobi, Kenya. I was eager to make a difference and eager to continue connecting with people around the world, rather than to entrench in isolationism. I found that volunteer medical missions were the ideal outlet for my energy. The number of missions for which I volunteered rose arithmetically over the ensuing decade. To date I have participated in nearly fifty medical missions and don't see an end to my enthusiasm.

Lani: Please tell us more about the other roles you have taken on with Operation Smile, as well as your other philanthropic efforts.

Arash: In addition to the general pediatrician on the Operation Smile team, I have often been the team physician as I've had the occasion to study diseases of the developing world.

My other philanthropic efforts include missions with other organizations, including the Becky Fund and Turtle Will, for which I have great respect. In 2009 friends and I started the Yanez Barragan Ecuador Project, which provides medical and dental care for the underserved people of specific areas of central Ecuador. We hope to build a clinic there in the next few years.

Lani: How do you cope with the suffering, injury, illness and death of children in your line of work?

Arash: I always focus on the positive changes I can make in the world and try to note what may be done in the future to improve the lives of others. On a personal level, I turn to friends and loved ones for emotional support. I exercise in both individual and team sports for the sheer enjoyment of it, as well as for stress relief.

Lani: What advice would you have for others ready to commit to finding and performing meaningful work?

Arash: Find a path that feeds you emotionally, spiritually. Make a plan, but be flexible and allow that plan to change. Connect to others who are doing the work you find meaningful or who are like-minded in their goals. Exchange ideas and learn from them. Work together in a team, if possible, and your efforts will multiply.

Time is the ultimate commodity. If you care about something, give to it your time, and it will invariably give back to you. Link your past with your present and future. Give to the things from which you have received. Your life is a painting, and each day is a stroke on that canvas, so come up with your own daily personal goals.

Lani: Thank you so much for your time.

Arash: The honor and pleasure to share these experiences is all mine, Lani.

It has been a joy to remain friends with Arash over the years, not only because he is a genuinely kind and loving person with a penchant for bad puns and a passion for helping others, but because he is someone who I feel truly personifies meaningful work. He volunteers his free time in service of a greater calling. It is not just a noble calling, but it also gives him a sense of connection to the larger world and a personal and professional sense of activism. If each of us could volunteer even just one hour a week of our time towards a cause we believe in and care about, just imagine how the world would change for the better.

My Jobs Over the Years and How They Led Me to My Calling

Over the years, I have worked in the fast food industry throughout high school, in cafés and retail stores during college and, later, as an English teacher at schools, community colleges and universities, and as a crisis counselor and volunteer coordinator at non-profit organizations. The common thread that linked all of these experiences was meaningful interactions.

In particular, even though the income was low, I loved working as a teacher. I have worked with people as young as four and as old as eighty and each experience also taught me about how people learn differently, myself included. Some of us are primarily visual learners. Some learn best by listening, while others are kinesthetic or physical learners. I also realized that our abilities to reason, create and perform may be hindered or enhanced by the setting as well as the expectations and education style of the teacher. The most difficult aspects of my teaching jobs were the need for discipline in the classroom, scoring stacks of papers and assigning grades. I could see the potential in all of my students and never liked failing a student, although there were times I did. The most meaningful part of teaching for me was when I saw a student "get it"; their face would light up and they became excited about the topic.

Even some of the most difficult jobs I've had were very meaningful. I learned a great deal about myself and other people through situations that were hierarchical, unethical and/or incredibly stressful. One job at which I only stayed for a couple of weeks was at a men's clothing store at a shopping mall, just before the holidays. Employees worked on commission, and I had made several large sales. As a result, I was expecting a significant bonus in my first paycheck. I found out, however, that the cashiers were directing other people's commissions to their friends. When I complained to the manager, he did nothing to address this situation, and I quit on the spot. This job taught me early on that my own self-worth was more important than any paycheck.

Another job that stands out was my experience at a domestic violence and sexual assault services center. I trained as a help line advocate, answering crisis phone calls and supporting survivors by sending out information and even filling out personal protection orders over the phone. The job itself was not stressful in the ways that I expected it to be. I expected to be concerned about survivors' safety, but I had been trained to handle those situations calmly and professionally. The main problem was that this non-profit organization had lost half its funding, due to an audit showing the previous director had misdirected donations over the course of a decade. Because of this mismanagement, programs and staff were cut, stress was very high, and morale was very low. People in this setting also tended to over-work and lack self-care. Nevertheless, the service I provided and the connections I made with clients and among my colleagues, some of whom I'm still in touch with today, made my time there valuable.

A job where I stuck it out through extremely difficult circumstances was as a volunteer coordinator at a local community college, a remedial program for students reading below college-level. While I was there, the new director fired three staff members one-by-one. She had been their colleague until she was promoted. We were all walking on eggshells after she announced that anyone in the department who was part-time could be "at-will" released for reason or no reason at all. My particular challenges were in maintaining a positive attitude and discretion with the volunteers while also being diplomatic and keeping my integrity intact during interactions with my boss and colleagues during what I half-jokingly in my mind called my boss' "Reign of Terror." For me, it was not so much that changes were made or that people were fired, as much as it was how they were made or fired: in secrecy and with seeming malice. Yet, my experiences and interactions with my boss at this job taught me that people who cause harm to others often think of themselves as victims and that they will strike out in order to prevent others from striking first. I also learned to keep my head, and to see things, people and events as they truly are, rather than how I wanted them to be. Ultimately, I learned that to be kind but unattached to any particular outcome was a wise choice, especially in the most arduous circumstances.

I did not know it then, but I have always been a life coach. The field of coaching was still in its infancy when I began my career. I learned through all of my work experiences that my surroundings might shift, that other people might see me and react differently to me depending on whatever role I was playing, but who I am—when I remember who I am—is someone who is compassionate, resilient and capable. I found my calling by following what held meaning for me in my work experiences: listening and caring about what other people had to say about their lives and how they wanted to change them. When I look back at all of the jobs I've had, they each taught me something important about myself, talents and skills and what I could offer the world.

According to *Attracting Perfect Customers: The Power of Strategic Synchronicity* by **Stacey Hall and Jan Brogniez:**

> Each of us, and the businesses we've joined or created, exists for a specific purpose or mission. Our businesses have developed as a result of our own experiences and needs and are simply tools for fulfilling our missions. Each business has its own mission to serve a particular group of customers in a particular way. That is why businesses have no need to compete with each other in the way we've traditionally thought of competition. Instead, business owners and managers could collaborate in ways that truly serve their customers' and their own interests.[22]

We are each here for a reason. Part of our life mission is to discover what that greater purpose is. Often people in business believe they are in competition with other businesses. The truth is that there are perfect customers for all businesses. Through all of my work experiences, I learned that I could actually serve clients better when I referred clients who were not a good fit for me or my business to other businesses who were a good fit. That's not to say I don't advertise or network or do outreach, but I don't worry about "the competition." I also discovered that the clients who were meant to work with me find me. Often my clients are people who are fully ready to step into their callings: work that they know they want to do and are really good at and which makes them and others happy. I work on making my own work meaningful. I focus on cooperation and collaboration with aligned people and businesses. I create coPOWERment.

Remembering who you are and what really matters to you will also provide a reliable and steady compass during any challenging work situation. We make meaning in our lives. Events occur. Other people interact with us. We tend to our duties, goals and dreams. However, the key thing to ask ourselves is "What (and who) really matters?" Every interaction can be made meaningful. Every action counts. No matter what we are doing to pay the bills, or in our relationships with others, what matters is whether and how we appreciate them everyday.

Meaningful Work Explorations:

If you have 5 to 10 minutes, answer the following:

What are the most important things that you want to gain from your job? (e.g. income, sense of accomplishment, title, ability to be promoted, calling, etc...)

Why are these things important to you?

What are some ways that I could find a job that would match these priorities?

Whom can I ask for help and support during this job search?

What are your beliefs about work?

Are there any false "master assessments" about work that could be holding you back from your full potential? If so, what could these be, and how could you change them so they offer more flexibility for new potentials in the future?

If you have more time, answer the following:

List some of your best and worst jobs here. What qualities made them positive or negative experiences for you? (e.g. friendly co-workers, good pay, opportunities to learn, etc…)

See if you can discover something that you learned from each job, and write it down here. What was meaningful about each work experience? What skills did you develop?

Most of us would like work, which tests our abilities and teaches us new skills but does not overwhelm us. Most would say they prefer a work environment where co-workers are friendly and there is a respectful and professional relationship between workers and supervisors. Most would also like work that pays well above sustainability level and offers opportunities for advancement. While these goals are important to keep in mind, there is, of course, no perfect job, and each of us will face difficulties or crises at work from time to time. Given these facts, what qualities will you look for in your future job searches?

Becoming a Parent

I take a very practical view of raising children. I put a sign in each of their rooms: "Checkout Time is 18 years."
–Erma Bombeck

Parenting 101?

One of the most challenging roles I have ever taken on is that of being a parent. In truth, like anything else, parenting is what you make of it. Whether I am able to stay in each moment—whether I worry about the future or dwell on the past—impacts my ability consistently to be a "good parent," that is, one who nurtures, guides and accepts my child for who he is.

My co-parenting partner, Justin, and I waited to have children. We had been married fifteen-and-a-half years before we even considered becoming parents. We knew it was a valuable and worthwhile experience, as many of our friends and family members had become parents over the years, but we just weren't certain we were ready for that level of responsibility in our twenties and thirties. Besides, like many people of our generation, we wanted to establish our careers, travel and enjoy each other's company first, before fully devoting ourselves to the care and upbringing of a little one. In addition chronic pain from a back injury in my thirties also physically postponed parenthood for me. It wasn't until I was thirty-nine that I had recovered sufficiently and became pregnant with our son, Noa.

We had worked on getting pregnant for a full year before it finally happened. It was emotionally, physically and spiritually strenuous at times, especially when we wanted it so badly. My doctor put it best when she said that it could be especially difficult for older women who have been successful in other aspects of their lives. "A woman may set the goal of pregnancy and expect to achieve it within a few months," she warned, "but nature doesn't always work that way." I tried to maintain perspective and optimism, but there were many times that I felt lost or like a failure when I didn't conceive right away. I noticed how my own unrealistic expectation that I would be able to become pregnant within half a year and the societal pressure impacted me. The roller coaster ride of thinking you're pregnant one month, only to discover you're not, was agonizing. I felt vulnerable in a way that I don't usually feel, a deep void in my womb, and I could be brought to tears by off-hand or thoughtless comments by family, friends or acquaintances. Some people even suggested that "waiting too long" was "our own fault" and that not being parents in our youth was somehow "selfish," while others merely shook their heads in sympathy. We can always adopt, I would console myself with this thought. Then, at the point when I was just about to let go and accept that it wasn't going to happen, it did.

I remember the weekend in October 2008 when we finally had a positive result on the home pregnancy test. I couldn't believe my eyes. There, in the little window of the plastic stick, was a plus symbol! I took the test again the next day just to be certain. Plus! On the following Monday I went to my doctor's office to have a blood test. I felt chilled even though it was warm that day. I was exhausted, slightly nauseated and very emotional that first couple of months, but I was also full of hope, and almost anything could make me smile.

I read all the latest books on pregnancy and delivery and was also given all kinds of unsolicited suggestions and tips by close friends and family. Strangers would say: "Eat an apple a day and you won't become constipated." "Don't eat brie or blue cheese." "Do some sort of exercise every day." Most of the advice was helpful. "Don't sleep on your side; sleep propped up on pillows!" "Don't sleep propped up on pillows; sleep on your side!" "I had a horrendous experience! Let me tell you!" Although many of the personal stories were positive, some people shared frightening and heartrending tales of miscarriage, excruciating deliveries, post-partum depression and birth defects. When I got the sense a conversation was heading in that direction, I would ask them if their story had a positive ending, and if it didn't, to please stop, because I was trying to maintain a peaceful and hopeful attitude. When I received contradictory advice, I would merely smile and say, "Thank you." People are so certain they are right about their opinions on childbirth and childrearing, more so than on any other topic, and complete strangers feel it is their right—nay duty!—to tell you what you should or shouldn't be doing as a pregnant woman and mother. However, one advantage to being an older mom is that I've already learned that I can't and shouldn't try to please everyone, and that it's also okay to sidestep an argument. Still, all this information and advice could never completely prepare me for what was to come.

Having a child is truly the most intimate connection I have ever had with another human being. My baby was dependent on me for his nutrition and well-being in-utero for almost 40 weeks; the umbilical cord connecting us in blood, body and, I believe, spirit. I was careful of what I ate, drank and breathed in. Even herbal tea, which used to be a favorite of mine on cold winter nights, had to be foregone in favor of hot water and lemon or specially formulated pregnancy tea, because I couldn't be certain the herbs I usually drank would be completely safe for a developing fetus. I exercised every day, alternately doing prenatal yoga, strength training and cardiovascular training on an elliptical machine. I imagined all the good things I was doing for my own health being transferred to my growing baby.

Would he be born with strong muscles? Would he be immune to the predisposition to diabetes, high blood pressure, alcoholism and depression that runs through both my partner's and my families? Would he like spicy food as much as I do? I had never thought of it in these terms before, but a pregnant woman is an infant's entire universe.

My partner loved and supported me throughout the pregnancy and birth, as he has throughout our lives together. Yet, there was a deepening in our relationship, a subtle understanding that this experience was something profound. We had had a cat for fifteen years, but her feline independence in no way compared to the absolute dependency of a young human being. People told us in generalizations, "Having a baby will change your lives completely, but it's worth it." Yet, words like these fail to convey the comprehensive shift in focus, time and energy when Justin and I became new parents.

The most obvious change was the need to be physically present for Noa when he was a baby and toddler. I loved being home with Noa the first couple of years, and I was fortunate to be able to arrange my work schedule around that priority. I loved being able to respond to his needs, but there were moments when I couldn't eat or go to the bathroom or take care of my own basic needs, because his needs—to be fed, changed or comforted—were more urgent. And I remember being constantly completely exhausted. No one ever tells you this. Another thing they don't tell you is that you feel like you've trained for the Olympic parenting event, but there are no medals or product endorsements for winning. And, finally, you feel like you've joined a special parenting club. When you meet another parent, there's a knowing glance (but no secret handshake) that passes between those who have experienced the intense fatigue, daily accountability and extreme joys of parenting.

Parenting As a Meditative Practice

There are moments when I catch myself repeating phrases my parents said to me, "It's okay," being one of them, when Noa is crying, angry or upset. No doubt their parents also said this to them. I've realized how this invalidates his feelings. When he has a dirty diaper or is hungry or exhausted, he's not okay, and it's okay for him not to be okay in that moment. So, instead, when I notice and catch myself, I've begun to say, "I can see you're sad/angry/upset/tired, but *it's going to be okay.*" For me, this subtle shift in my language and awareness of what I am saying, not to mention *how* I am saying it, is crucial in respecting his right to feel the full range of his emotions and to be present with the full range of his experiences.

Although parental fatigue and responsibility are, indeed, heavy at times, there are moments of pure bliss: when Noa learns something new, and he smiles or laughs out loud. Parenting has taught both Justin and myself what is most important to each of us in life. Our child's growth, learning and well-being are a priority, as are, on a larger scale, working towards creating a better world in which he and other children will grow up. While it's more difficult to make and keep appointments and to plan and follow through with social events and gatherings as a parent than when I was not, my typical routines and schedules have been replaced with a go-with-the-flow philosophy: parenting, the ideal awareness practice.

Parenting Explorations:

If you are a parent:
If you have 5 to 10 minutes, answer the following:

What is the one thing that is most important to you about your role as a parent?

What factors contributed to your parenting choices?

What do you wish you had known earlier about being a parent?

If you have more time, answer the following:

How has having a child changed your life?

What would you share with other parents about the challenges and joys of parenting?

What resources have you and your partner found helpful in raising your child?

Create a parenting collage or keepsake box of mementos. You can decorate these with colored paper, ribbon, cloth or whatever strikes your fancy. Then add a copy of the child's birth certificate, hand and foot prints, photographs, journal entries, booties, school artwork or report cards and any other items that represent your unique relationship and role as a parent to your child. Keep this someplace special, where you can cherish it and share it with friends and family, if you wish.

If you are not a parent:
If you have 5 to 10 minutes, answer the following:

What prevented or has postponed parenthood for you?

What factors contributed to your choices?

What do you wish you had known earlier about these choices?

If you have more time, answer the following:

How has not having a child affected your life?

What would you share with others about the challenges and joys of choosing not to become a parent?

Are there other parental-like roles that you have had (i.e. caregiver, mentor, teacher) that have held special meaning for you? How have these roles enriched your life and the lives of others?

Lost and Found

*So if you really want to help this world,
what you will have to teach is how to live in it.
And that no one can do who has not themselves
learned how to live in the joyful sorrow and
sorrowful joy of the knowledge of life as it is.*
–Joseph Campbell

Lost and Found?

As you read the title to this chapter, you probably thought of objects or things that you have lost: a trinket, an heirloom or maybe even friendships or other relationships. Yet, there are so many ways that we ourselves are lost and found. We might discover that what we thought was true is not true. We could discover that what we thought was reality is not real. We may discover that who we are is more than who we thought we were, more than just a title or a role we play. Sometimes what we lose is an old version of ourselves. Or we might lose our faith, our dreams or old beliefs. By losing our former ways of seeing things, the old ways of being, we discover freedom. With courage, perseverance and hope, we can find our true selves and a sense of purpose.

A Calling to Serve

I created and started facilitating Creating CoPOWERment® Workshops, LLC in Ann Arbor, Michigan in August 2005. These workshops came out of a time in my life a few years before when everything had fallen apart. My back had been badly injured in 1999 due to overwork and a lack of self-care, and it took me almost a decade to recover fully. For a time I lost my health, my employment, some friends and, almost, my life. Work, relationships and friendships were forever transformed, and I realized that I needed to choose how I was going to frame this injury experience in my life. I could view it as a great tragedy, which, of course, it was. I could view it as an amazing opportunity, which it also was. The truth is that it was both.

There were things I needed to lose, a certain way of being hard-working, self-sacrificing and over-giving, the way I was brought up, in order to find a more authentic self and way of being. The spinal injury seemed to be an indication of how "out of alignment" I was in the rest of my life. I lost a lot, but in return I also found my true calling.

My own painful transition served as a wake-up call to serve others going through transition and transformation. I support others going through changes in their lives by encouraging them to explore how they currently spend their time, what they would rather be devoting their time to and to ask themselves if this is in alignment. I assist clients with creative life re-design.

I also offer an opportunity for people to visualize their ideal lives by creating a concrete "Vision Collage," in which images taken from catalogs and magazines are then pasted on a folder, a catch file, for the ideal self. By seeing these images on paper (not only in black and white or gray but also in color), people rediscover for themselves what it is they truly want in their lives. They can see exactly how much time is spent worrying or commuting or doing things that do not fulfill them, as well as where they would like to scale back or expand particular activities. Seeing their dreams spread out on a folder, clients can begin to see how it is possible to create this ideal life. They can begin to devote themselves to their ideal lives by asking themselves who else can and will support them through these changes, what they can do today, next week, next month, this year to bring their current choices in alignment with their ideal lives. They also explore why they have not yet already made changes, what is holding them back.

In short, my clients begin to draw up a plan for change, with some basic guidelines and ideas. Then they can adjust course as needed and create a new plan if necessary. In further sessions we explore mindful movement with full awareness and emotional balance, as well as community coPOWERment or how to align with local, national and international communities with similar goals and priorities.

In America we're taught to set goals, to strive for some particular outcome, to believe that if we work hard enough and sacrifice long enough, we will reach our goals, be successful and live happily ever after. Life doesn't always work this way. It's much better than that! Most people already know what they want out of life and how they might fit best in the larger scheme of things. They're just not always sure how to go about creating it. Sometimes when things don't go according to our plans, we forget that maybe those plans weren't in alignment with what we're really meant to be doing. Obstacles arise, situations aren't always what they seem and other people are also trying to find their way. After five years of service in Ann Arbor, Michigan, I opened Creating CoPOWERment® Center, LLC in Honolulu, Hawai'i, specializing in transitional and transformational empowerment workshops and coaching. That was something I could never have imagined happening without the things I lost and found along the way.

An Interview with Michael Purcell
Professional Artist

michael.purcell.1276@facebook.com

A dear friend of mine, Michael Purcell, is a professional artist. He paints. His styles include cubism, surrealism and other abstract styles, and like many creative people I know, he is always stretching himself, experimenting, never content to rest on his laurels.

I first met Michael through another friend on Facebook. I was impressed by his witty responses, his unique perspective, so I friended him. I give all my friends nicknames; certain aspects of their personalities, spirit and humor reveal themselves as I get to know them. Michael's nickname is "Magical." Little did I know how accurate that nickname would be.

I met Michael in person for the first time in Denver, October 2011. I was in Colorado, attending a coaching training conference through Newfield Network. There was an instant sense of connection, a sort of recognition. I have experienced this a few times in my life when the idea of reincarnation seems to be confirmed at a deep level. When I met Michael, face-to-face, I remember thinking, "Oh, it's so nice to see you again!"

Magical lived in a one-bedroom apartment in uptown Denver, not far from the Ogden Theater and Hamburger Mary's. I normally would not agree to meet a "stranger" at his home, but Michael's apartment and studio were one and the same, and I wanted to see the paintings he had posted on Facebook, up close and in person. I drove to Denver from Boulder, navigating one-way streets with GPS to a blond brick, three-story building on the corner. I parked the car on the street and got my bearings.

Magical Michael is six feet tall and svelte. He resembles what I imagine Anne Rice's Vampire Lestat would look like:

elegant and handsome in a somewhat dangerous way. He was wearing black jeans and a dress shirt with long sleeves and dress shoes. In one of his Facebook photos, he had worn a black top hat and carried a crystal-topped cane. Even though he did not have those accessories with him at that moment, they left such an indelible impression, I somehow remember him wearing them even though I know this was not the case.

We embraced and said hello, then walked up a short flight of steps to his first floor apartment. The hallway walls had not been repainted in some time, but the space was clean. Fluorescent lights flickered overhead. Michael opened the door to his place, and my first impressions were of art, multiple canvases of all sizes and colors, stacked against the walls, arrangements of odds and ends like in an old-fashioned curiosity shop and the pungent aroma of what I would later discover were Pall Mall cigarettes.

"Would you like a cup of coffee?" He had a smoker's voice, scratchy and deeply resonant. I accepted, even though it was early evening, and I normally have just one cup in the morning.

Michael's furnishings were modest but well-cared for: a sofa covered with an afghan, a chair, easels and a worktable. I sat in the chair and noticed a grey tabby cat who sauntered into the living room. Kitty came up to meet my acquaintance while Magical was in the kitchen. She was about half the size of most other cats I've known. I murmured to her as I stroked her fur, and she rubbed against my jeans. I looked up and saw a blue velvet curtain suspended between the living room and kitchen and a sign that read: "The Time Is Near," which could be interpreted several ways, and it intrigued me. There were several paintings of his displayed on the walls in vivid colors and dark and light tones. One, in particular, caught my eye. It took up half the wall and was beige and gold with the outline of a man inside the shadow of a woman, with what looked like white strobe lights running the perimeter.

"Michael, what's that painting called?" I asked, as he strode into the living room with my coffee.

He followed my line of sight and replied, "Man Inside Woman."

"Perfect!" I exclaimed. I would later buy that painting and arrange to have it shipped to Honolulu.

Magical stood to one side and put a CD in on the sound system. I can't remember now what song he played, but his tastes are eclectic, and it could have been Cole Porter or Johnny Cash or the Smiths.

"You like it?" he asked, one side of his mouth higher than the other, bemused and at the same time flattered.

"Very much," I said. "You know I love your art."

Michael sat on the sofa opposite me, and the kitty immediately hopped up to be petted. By the way he stroked the cat, I could tell he was a caring person. His caresses were intended for the feline's maximum benefit, and he spoke to her lovingly. I could hear her purring.

"So…," I asked, "how long have you lived in Denver?"

"Eight years," he replied, rolling his eyes a little. "You sound thrilled." I laughed.

"Oh, I like it all right, but it's not like San Francisco or New York." He tapped his cigarette into the ashtray and took a sip of his coffee. The cat curled up behind him on the sofa like a lumbar support cushion. Magical proceeded to tell me about his time in both of those cities. He had been painting for over two decades, and prior to that, he had been a professional male model and waiter, but he had chosen to devote himself full-time to painting in 1995.

"What happened then?" I asked.

A shadow crossed over his face, and there was a moment of hesitation before he replied, "I found my calling, and I haven't looked back." He lit a cigarette then and took a long drag. "How about you?" he asked, changing the subject.

In respect for his obvious pain and my own eagerness to share, I told him my story. "In a nutshell…grew up in Hawai'i, lived in England, Colorado, California and Michigan before returning back home to Honolulu to live in 2010. Married 19 years, have a son, happily divorced and still friends with my ex-husband. I've been a teacher, writer, crisis counselor, and now I'm a life coach." I smiled, thinking how funny that a lifetime can be summed up so quickly. "Of course, you know a lot of that already from my posts."

Magical nodded, deep in his own thoughts, as he took another drag on his cigarette. He was prone to post photos of his paintings, as well as witty comments on Facebook like, "My birthday suit is at the cleaners," "Hell has come to Denver" and "Wash the dishes or throw them out?" while I was apt to post humorous forwards, family snapshots and thought-provoking quotations.

It was like visiting an old friend and catching up where we had left off, even though we had just met for the first time in person. It was miraculous. Even though I am usually allergic to cigarette smoke, there it did not bother me in the slightest. Another miraculous thing.

On the Value of "Dark Value"

Michael also teaches painting at his church. He started to tell me about a quality in good paintings, whereby the contrast between light and dark areas is extreme. This he called "dark value." Since I am not a painter, I was unfamiliar with this term, but I liked the idea as a writer.

"I'm always trying to get my students to see it and use it," he said, lighting another cigarette. "It's the most difficult thing for some of them to get. Dark value gives a painting depth, contrast and impacts the viewer."

I listened, sipping my coffee. It was good, strong coffee, and it warmed me from the inside out. Autumn in Colorado is pleasant, in the 60s typically, but dry and crisp enough for long pants and a leather jacket.

I sensed a sudden shift in Michael. His voice was lower, slower, as he began to describe how he became an artist. "I was a male model, went out practically every night. I had just moved from San Francisco to San Diego, of all places, and I was already painting full-time." He stood up and strode into the kitchen, placing his empty mug in the sink before returning. "That's when I got sick….It's not contagious," he assured me, before I even thought to ask.

"What happened?" I asked, tenderly.

"I can't believe I've lived with this for eleven years." Magical shook his head. "Some people kill themselves, the pain is so bad. And the worst part is that doctors don't know what causes it." Magical rolled back his long sleeves, and I could see several wounds, which had scabbed over on his forearms. He stared at me, expecting, perhaps, for me to be disgusted or upset or to show pity.

I felt none of those things, only compassion. My heart was open, and I was silent, allowing the pause to hang between us, but not in an uncomfortable way, more like a companionable silence between good friends.

Michael went on to describe how he felt an unbearable itching in his legs, at first, that felt like it went to the bone, then the rash broke out over his back, arms and neck. "It was horrible," he said, matter-of-factly. "I couldn't stop scratching, and none of the doctors could tell me what it was. All they know is it isn't contagious. Some of them think it's psychological." He flicked his long fingers, dismissing that theory in distaste. "It comes back frequently. Sometimes better, sometimes worse. I am scarred all over my body."

I could empathize, even though, of course, I couldn't fully understand how devastating this would be to a man who had once made a living as a model. I told Michael about my own experience with debilitating back pain. I had been injured at the age of 29 in 1999 at work, while tutoring a child with severe emotional and learning disabilities. The child had started banging his head against the wall, and I had reached out to stop him and pulled my shoulder and back out of alignment. "It was really symbolic of how else I was out of alignment in my life at that time," I said. "I was overworking, not taking good care of myself and driving long hours in heavy traffic in the Bay Area." I held my hands up as if in surrender. "And the rest is history."

We were both quiet for a moment. Music played, something jazzy yet soothing. "Do you realize that our injuries and illnesses happened at about the same time?" I asked.

"That *is* strange," Michael replied.

We sat in companionable silence, listening to the music.

"What is your…," I searched for the right word, "condition called?"

"Morgellon's disease," Michael replied.

I nodded, unfamiliar with it.

"There are treatments, but they haven't found a cure. It's been difficult." He paused, then said, "I haven't always handled it well. Depression, rage. I haven't always been myself." He waited, as if expecting me to say something, but I simply nodded and looked at him with kindness.

Sometimes while coaching clients, I've found that it's not so much the advice or insight I have to offer that is healing, as much as the willingness to genuinely listen. I have found that there is something sacred in bearing witness to someone else's suffering. I don't have to fix or change anything or "make it all better." I just need to care.

I could tell that Michael knew I cared about him, but I did not pity him. He had survived a devastating loss and yet continued to create beauty in spite...or maybe because...of it.

"I have done some horrible things...," he began and stopped.

"Who hasn't?" I said, tenderly.

He looked surprised by my response. The cat behind him got up and stretched, then hopped down and proceeded to groom herself, as we both watched her.

I spoke slowly and clearly and with as much love as I could muster, "Do you realize, Michael, that particular time in your life was *your* 'dark value'?"

He looked up at me, blinking.

"We all have our crosses to bear." I smiled at him and then said, "I'd say you were overdue for 11 years or more of happiness for a change."

He took in what I said.

Truthfully, I don't know where these words came from. I believe that when I am coaching or listening to a friend going through a hard time, when I speak with love, Spirit speaks through me. I believe that I am a channel for the highest good of all and that I can sometimes *see* into souls. I am deeply honored when clients or friends confide in me, and I know that they sense that I care.

When I was an adolescent, I read a book that had a profound impact on my life. I used to escape into other worlds in my childhood, because being in my parents' home was sad and depressing. The book which left such a lasting impression on me was *The Soul Singer of Tyrnos* by Ardath Mayhar.[23] It was a science fiction novel about a young woman whose calling was to sing a person's soul. Those who were unjust or cruel were revealed as scoundrels, and those who had lived well received the blessing of knowing they were on the right track. This book resonated with me like a bell rung in a cathedral. At the moment Michael and I were talking, I remembered this book, but I did not tell him about it until much later. I didn't want him to think I was crazy. I wanted to stay present with his story.

At the end of that first visit of many, Magical told me, "I wouldn't wish this on anyone, and I wish it would go away, but I have survived it with my art and spirituality, and because of it, I am stronger." He paused to stroke his feline companion, who rose up to meet his hand. "I am still depressed sometimes, and I am still in pain, but my life has value." He breathed in and out deeply, sighing.

"Dark value," I said, nodding, "and light…and everything in between." Magical Michael showed me that darkness is darkness, but it has value in our lives.

I told him later, "There is nothing to be ashamed of and nothing you can tell me that I can't handle or that would make me love you any less. Other people would benefit from knowing that, even going through the worst of it, and behaving in ways they aren't always proud of, there is light at the other end of the tunnel of trauma. They would benefit by knowing that it's still not easy, even now, but that you have found meaningful ways to cope and create beauty in your life in spite and *because* of it." It was after that, and after I had shared my own stories of darkness in my life, that he agreed to share his story of "dark value." I am grateful to him for his willingness to share his story with me and also with readers of this book, in order that we might understand that even the most devastating and painful of losses can lead to something precious found.

Lost and Found Explorations:

If you have 5 to 10 minutes, answer the following:

What have you lost in your life?

What have you found?

If you have more time, answer the following:

What meaning(s) did you make of these losses and discoveries?

How have these past experiences impacted who you are and who you want to be in the present?

Notice that how we interpret our experiences is actually more relevant than the experiences themselves? How we interpret our past experiences in the present impacts what we will do, say and think in the future. It influences what we think is possible.

Community CoPOWERment©:

This self-exploration offers a clear-cut procedure to consider where you may feel out of balance and may need more connection to others in your community. It helps you, first, to find ways to realign yourself and then to network with local, national and international communities that are meaningful to you. This will take ~20-30 minutes to complete.

1. Study the three-part balance of self in relation to community and the two dysfunctional extremes in the chart below. Assess where you believe you are *right now* in terms of your balance on this continuum and place a check mark there.

Balance of Self Worth and the Two Dysfunctional Extremes:

+ extreme (too much)	balanced	- extreme (too little)
Obsessive Wealth/ Entitlement	Abundance/ Security	Poverty/Lack of resources
Status/Prestige/ "Somebody"	Self-Respect/ Self-Esteem	Disrespect/ Unworthy/"Nobody"
"Beauty" at any cost	Self-Love/Self-Acceptance/Self-Compassion	Ugly/Undesirable
Control/Extreme Independence	Interdependence	Dependence/ Isolation

Abundance and security are balanced qualities, in which we feel our material needs are met, whereas obsession with wealth or feeling poverty-stricken are the dysfunctional extremes.

Self-respect and self-esteem are the normal, healthy balanced conditions for a sense of well-being, whereas the persistent need for status, prestige or to be a "somebody" at the expense of others or feeling disrespected, unworthy or a "nobody" are the two unhealthy extremes.

Self-love and self-acceptance are at the heart of knowing we have self-worth and can offer something valuable to our communities. The dysfunctional extremes, beauty at any cost and feeling ugly or undesirable, occur only when we are out of balance and are viewing ourselves from a distorted, exterior focus.

Finally, independence is overvalued in this culture at the expense of a more realistic and balanced need for interdependence (not to be confused with co-dependence). None of us is an island. We must depend on others at times and others must be able to rely on us. Therefore, interdependence is the balanced middle ground, while the hunger for control or extreme independence or the disempowering feelings of dependence or isolation are the dysfunctional extremes. Community coPOWERment occurs in interdependent situations. When we realize that we are in each moment worthy of our own love and acceptance, we will discover ways we can pay that forward to others. It is only when we find our own balance that we can offer something beneficial to others in our communities.

2. Review of Balance

Envision what each of these would mean for you. If it is already in balance, simply write "balanced" and move on to another. Write a definition for each; in other words, how would each of these needs manifest in your life if they were habitual? Be as specific as possible:

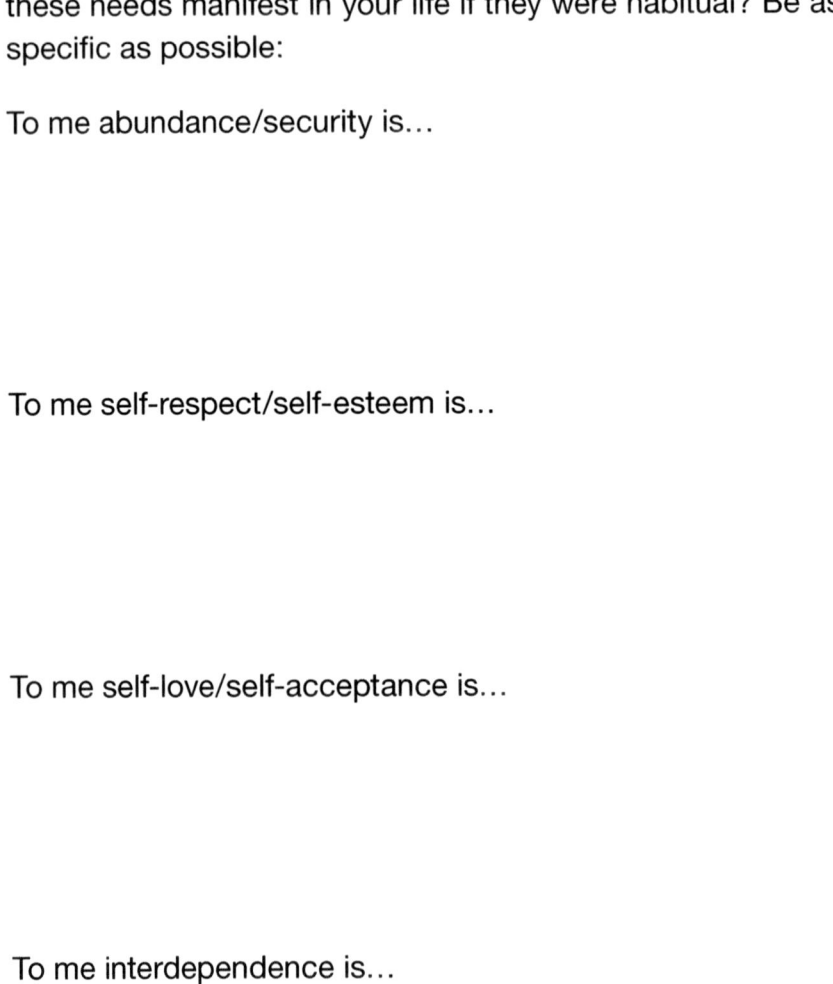

To me abundance/security is…

To me self-respect/self-esteem is…

To me self-love/self-acceptance is…

To me interdependence is…

3. Restoring Balance

Consider *when, why and how* you may have gotten out of balance for each of these normal, balanced needs. If it is already in balance, simply write "balanced" and move on to another.

Abundance/security: *When/Why/How* out of balance:

Self-respect/self-esteem: *When/Why/How* out of balance:

Self-love/self-acceptance: *When/Why/How* out of balance:

Interdependence: *When/Why/How* out of balance:

4. Personal Realignment Action Plan:

What would you need to do to return to balance in each area of your life? Approximately how much time might you need? You can take small short-term steps and/or plan larger, longer-term goals here. *This is a space to brainstorm and consider all of your options before selecting ones you actually would like to implement.* If you need more space, feel free to use another piece of paper or write on the back.

For a sense of abundance/security, I want to: ~ Amount of time needed:

For a sense of self-respect/self-esteem, I want to: ~ Amount of time needed:

For a sense of self-love/self-acceptance, I want to: ~ Amount of time needed:

For a sense of interdependence, I want to: ~ Amount of time needed:

5. Networking and Community CoPOWERment©:

Who can you ask for advice about living with meaningful community connections?

List names here, as well as how, when and where you plan to connect with them. Consider connecting via e-mail or phone or in person at an event. Or, perhaps, you could invite these people to lunch or coffee? Ask friends and family about their connections to people doing the kinds of volunteer work, community networking or co-powering enterprises in which you are interested.

Name(s) of contact(s)   How/When/Where to contact:

What kinds of communities would you like to be a part of locally, nationally and/or globally? Why? If you're not certain about names of particular organizations, then simply write down types or themes of groups that you would like to be part of (e.g. racial equality, environmental activism, women's rights, religious/spiritual affiliations, etc…).

How you would like to utilize your talents, skills or resources to support these groups? In what ways could they support and/or inspire you?

Living Your Full Potential

Forgiveness Is Not Forgetting

*Courageous people do not fear forgiving,
for the sake of peace.*
–Nelson Mandela

Forgiveness is Not Forgetting

Forgiveness is not forgetting. It is a fact that people sometimes do or say horrible things to one another. Like wild animals we fight, flee or freeze when we are under attack. We act and react, yet it is how we choose to interpret our own or others' behaviors that truly impacts us. Awareness allows us, over time, to forgive, even if we do not, cannot, and, in some cases, must not forget.

Forgiveness is Spirit's gift to humanity. It takes us from the level of wild animal to conscious being. It allows people in worthwhile relationships to heal, to reconcile and to move forward. In forgiving, we see that we too have been unstable or unhappy or unconscious at times in our lives and that we have said or done something we regret, at least once to another person and probably to someone we love. We can understand how others find themselves in difficult circumstances or make poor choices or rash decisions. We can choose to have compassion for ourselves and for others because, quite frankly, being human can be rough sometimes.

Forgiveness, like the truth, sets us free.

I have always been the kind of person who lifts up a scab before it has fully healed. I'll rinse the wound in clean water, pat it dry, add extra antibiotic cream, another bandage, all the while reminding myself that it takes time to heal, and I should just leave it be. Inevitably, I still pick at my wounds. This must have something to do with being a writer.

Writers have a never-ending desire to see through illusion to the heart of things. We are observers. We try to put the enigmatic and sublime into words. We try to make the nonsensical make some sort of sense. We try to fit the pieces of the puzzle into place. We bring the truth to the light through the shadows of falsehood. We make whole what once was fractured. Feelings, thoughts and motivations of characters, narration and point of view, setting and plot intrigue me and compel me in stories and in real life. Yet, paradoxically, writers also tend to like double entendre, symbolism and irony: the ambiguity of words and the ambivalence of life. Writers like complexity.

My ex-husband and best friend, Justin Meilgaard, is not a writer, but he is my editor. He makes certain I make sense. He edits my work for punctuation, grammar and, most importantly, content. He is still the first to see my early drafts and the first to pick up copies of the final printed editions to share with others. For over twenty years, he was a study abroad adviser to college students wishing to study overseas, as well as to international students who came to the U.S. for a semester or a year. He advised them on courses to take, how to avoid being mugged and how to deal with culture shock and respect the traditions of the host country. Now he manages professor room assignments, tenure track and building issues for a Dean's office. Justin is pragmatic. He knows that problems will arise, difficulties will rear their ugly heads from time to time and challenges will occur.

Justin has taught me the most about forgiveness of anyone I know. He has forgiven me several times in our friendship, which has spanned over two decades now. He forgave me when I said something hurtful to him in a moment of anger, when I foolishly got involved with an abusive man mid-way through our marriage in a moment of madness and when I hurt us both deeply. He has taught me that it's okay to make mistakes, as long as you learn from them and take the time, energy and steps to remedy the situation. He has also taught me that some mistakes can never be taken back but that we can still do our best to change for the better after making them, never to repeat them and to make amends to those we hurt.

As for me, I have taught Justin to take more risks, to have some fun and to be willing to perform without a safety net sometimes. I also tend to be his counselor in tough situations, helping him to navigate emotional white water and bailing him out of trouble spots. And I, too, have forgiven him many times: for late nights at the office, for forgetting what I said just a few moments before and for continually taking his father's side over my own, which, though in due course it damaged our marriage, could not end our friendship.

I recently asked him why, after all these years and the ups and downs, he has chosen to co-parent a child with me as we are entering our forties, when most people our age are looking into college for their offspring. His response? "I want you in my life. You make life fun." As for me, Justin makes life calm. Even though we are no longer married, with our son, Noa, we are a family.

Another Relationship in which to Practice Forgiveness

Recently I have been faced with a situation in which it is much more difficult to forgive.

I struggled with how to tell this story, as I am concerned with the ethics of sharing the details of other people's private lives. Even in this age of tell-all media, "reality" shows and paparazzi, I believe that people have a right to keep portions of their lives private. So I decided to tell this story only as it pertains to my own life but, of course, we are all interconnected, and my story does not make sense in isolation. Before publishing it I contacted all of the members of my family. I e-mailed them this chapter in order to gain some perspective, to ask for their support and to receive their advice and feedback. As I mentioned before in the chapter, "Is Your Glass Half Full or Empty?," Truth with a capital "T" is made up of multiple perspectives. Events occur, other people act and react, but the interpretations of what and why things happened will be vastly different, depending upon whom you ask.

My father was not an active part of my life growing up. I really didn't know him well. The only times I saw him were on weekends, when we would drive to the beach or the mountains, or when we travelled on family vacations, summer or Christmas trips to visit my grandparents. I have some happy memories of family times together: bar-be-ques at the beach, going to see movies like *Star Wars*, *Labyrinth* and *Close Encounters of the Third Kind*, Disneyland, board games like Monopoly and Clue and Dad surprising my mother, sisters and me with tickets to see Shaun Cassidy in concert at the Blaisdell Arena, because he was my first crush when I was about seven or eight years old.

Yet, most of the time, my father was not at home. My recollection was that Dad was constantly working. He worked full-time and overtime at Pearl Harbor Shipyard and also at other part-time jobs, as a mechanic and delivering pizza, to support the family. This is not unusual in Hawaiʻi, where the cost of living is higher and wages are lower than in the continental U.S. It was also not that unusual for men of the 1970s and '80s to be the primary breadwinner. The problem was, much of his income was spent on other people, partying with friends and not coming home over several days, when I was very young. Later, when he became a Christian, the spending was on other people and projects at his church. Mom often bemoaned this and resented the pressure she felt he was putting on her to find a job outside the home, when she was already overwhelmed with three daughters and all of the household chores.

My parents later opened a doll and miniature store in 'Aiea, which eventually went out of business. They never fully recovered from this blow. I was also sexually assaulted at this time, as I mentioned earlier in this book. It was a turning point in our family, after which each member became more and more distant and isolated from each other. My parents tried family psychotherapy, but the counselor labeled us "dysfunctional," and she seemed to take sides. It was too much for my parents to deal with, and they were unwilling to accept responsibility for their issues. They cancelled future appointments. Only my sister, Lea, and I were close, and I attribute that closeness to our ability to survive the instability, to become more resilient to it and eventually to escape.

In more than just one way, we were always just barely scraping by.

I remember my mother sobbing as she added up the tens of thousands in debt that they owed to various creditors. She would sometimes borrow birthday or Christmas money from my sisters and me to pay for the groceries, or else ask for help from her father. We could never afford the down payment for a home. I remember my mother saying, "Don't tell your other grandparents about what is happening." It was as if by ignoring their own pain and shame, my parents thought it would somehow go away. However, keeping secrets only made things worse.

There was a lingering shadow of unhappiness, instability and deep-seated, unvoiced shame in the people who were supposed to be raising me. My parents themselves had had challenging childhoods. My mother had grown up wearing glasses and was overweight. She was teased relentlessly, but she was also smart, witty and creative and graduated from a business school. My father had a challenging time keeping up in school, but he had been a talented clarinet player and earned a music scholarship to Redlands University, which is when he met my mother. Then he was drafted to fight in Vietnam.

I inherited both their creativity and trauma. As soon as I was fifteen, I went to school full-time, as well as working part-time to pay for my own expenses. I left home as soon as I was able to, by earning a full-ride scholarship at the University of Hawai'i and working part-time at sales jobs in college. After graduating and getting married, I would call my parents a few times a year, visit every other year and send gifts at birthdays and Christmas, even though they often forgot about Justin and me. Yet, Justin reminded me that my dad had also gifted each daughter $5000 after he retired from Pearl Harbor Shipyard, at a time when we really needed it. My parents' attention and love was unreliable and sporadic, but at least it was there.

Then the disaster struck in 2000. They would go on about it over the phone, "We just have to put up the initial investment. No need to be involved after." Red flashing lights and warning sirens were blaring in my head. I felt a terrible sense of foreboding, like an ice cold enema surging through my guts. "But what do you know about truck stops? "What do you know about this partner of yours?" "Why does he need your credit to invest in this opportunity?" My concerns and advice to be cautious were ignored, as they always had been. My parents lost their investment and were even further in debt. Then they were being physically threatened by the con man. They fled to a motel. At this point I would call them daily, concerned for their well-being.

Then, one day I called, and they had checked out without telling me. Worse, when I finally did reach them, they did not understand why I was so upset. They were so wrapped up in their own trauma that they had no comprehension of how their poor choices were impacting my sisters and me. This is when I understood fully that I had been parenting my parents for years, and that it had to stop.

Fast forward ten years, and our relationship was distant but caring. They had moved in with my grandfather, when he needed someone to care for him as he recovered from chemotherapy. They later inherited his house when he died. I requested that we keep in touch by writing only. It was draining to listen to my mother list all of her grievances on the phone, to hear her rant about what the latest mistake was that my father had made, how often she forgave him, about how he was donating money they didn't have to the church, how she was doing all kinds of craft and art projects, buying books and supplies with money they didn't have, her saying how proud she was of me and my sisters, then in the same breath lamenting that we weren't closer.

In 2010 Justin, Noa and I visited my parents. They had not yet met their grandson. I felt an obligation to allow this connection, as my parents were the only living grandparents that Noa still had, even though they had not made an effort to visit me while I was pregnant or after I gave birth. Friends of mine thought it very odd. I was used to it. I loved my parents but it was difficult to be close to them.

We had just moved from Ann Arbor, Michigan to Honolulu, Hawai'i in March of that year. We also had the familial obligation of returning Justin's father's ashes to Denmark just a few months prior in June. I was exhausted. Yet, still, we flew to LAX on Labor Day weekend and had lunch at Sizzler in San Bernardino, CA. It had been ten years since I had seen them, and I was astounded by how worn out my parents looked. My mother, in particular, was grey. The restaurant was packed, and other families' conversations provided white noise, interrupted by the sounds of clattering silverware. Sizzler lived up to its name, as the aroma of sizzling beef, chicken and seafood wafted through the restaurant. I picked at my salad. My back ached.

Conversation with my parents was stiff and dealt mostly with how big Noa

was getting. "He's a rice sack!" Dad said. "Potato sack," Mom replied. Noa just laughed. He was learning how to walk and toddled unsteadily but purposefully towards my parents. He sensed he was adored and knew innately that all he had to do was be himself and soak it all up. His gait resembled my mother's in a paradoxical way. My mother was limping due to a spider bite that had become infected, and, because she was diabetic, it had required a stay at the hospital to recover. I remember thinking, *I'm so glad I planned this trip. I'm not sure how long Mom will be here.* One of the last things she said to me, as she always did in closing was, "Be a good girl." To which I replied, "Mom, I prefer to be human."

Later I would hear secondhand by phone and e-mail via my middle sister, Lea, anything requiring urgent assistance: time and money needed to reorganize the house, the need to talk with my father about my mother's failing health, Lea's fear that my parents had become those people on an episode of *Hoarders*. Then my mother passed away in June 2012. Lea told me later that Mom had known she needed a heart valve replacement for three years but did not schedule surgery to fix it.

I was numb.

After nine months of intensive life coach training, I was graduating from Newfield Network, one of the top coaching programs in the world, in Denver, Colorado. It wasn't too difficult to reroute through southern California first, but it was painful. *How typical.* I couldn't help thinking, feeling badly even as I did, *Whenever something is going well for me there's guaranteed to be bad news from them.* I know that my mother couldn't have foreseen my graduation would be within a week of her funeral, and I felt ashamed at resenting her for ruining my happiness, yet again.

In addition my father could not afford a funeral. My mother's body was at the hospital, then taken to a funeral home to be cremated. Could we, the three daughters, pay for the cremation and funeral and attend in a few weeks time? My father said he would arrange for everything. It would cost each daughter $1000. My father didn't ask as much as he seemed to expect we would follow through. He let us know the weekend before the funeral home required the money to proceed. We emergency wired the funds. How could I not agree to such a request? To do so would mean leaving my mother's body at the funeral home until someone else could pay to claim it. I thought about my mother, the times she did her best to make sure that my sisters and I learned how to cook, clean, take care of ourselves, put on makeup and to make art. No, she didn't deserve that.

Fast forward again. The funeral, attended by family who flew in from Maui, Washington, California and Massachusetts, members of my father's church, my sisters and me. It was beautiful: floral arrangements, tasteful beige décor and subdued lighting, a slide show and even music my aunts and uncles performed live with my father at the front of the San Bernardino memorial building. My mother's mortal remains were in a wooden box the size of a toaster. I remember little of it, except a feeling of relief that it was over and gratitude that I didn't need to handle it on my own. I delivered a eulogy on my sisters' and my behalf about how my mother had been an artist and mother, creative and talented, saddened by the hardships she had faced, yet still loved.

This wasn't a time to go into too much detail. No need to mention to the aunts and uncles that Lea, Laura and I had paid for the funeral. Besides, my father, as always, couldn't keep his hair clean or combed. His clothes were even more stained and wrinkled than usual. He didn't seem to understand basic social cues, like why it was inappropriate to buy a new banjo when he was filing for bankruptcy and play it out loud in a restaurant. We all thought, *He's grieving.* Yet, it wasn't until later that I realized how severely irrational his behavior could be.

During the following months he began e-mailing my sisters and myself weekly about his loneliness, his problems, his daily tasks. He never once asked how we were doing, not even his grandson. It was overwhelming and frightening. He demanded that my sisters pay for a plane ticket and house him, so he could spend Thanksgiving with them in Northern California. They didn't feel they could refuse a widower in mourning, even though neither of them could afford the extra expense.

Then came the announcement. My father said he had met a woman on ChristianMingle.com just one month before in January, just six months after my mother's death, yet was planning to marry her one month later on Valentine's Day. "Are you crazy?!" I wrote to him among several other less kind words. It wasn't so much that he wanted to remarry. He was an adult. But why so soon? And why to someone he had just met online? Did she know about the bankruptcy? What was she getting out of it? My sister, Lea, was more diplomatic, e-mailing: "Wouldn't it be better to take more time to be certain and to get to know each other first?" My girlfriends speculated that he had known her for a longer time and that the dating site story was a ruse. It didn't really matter, though, did it? It was yet another disaster, yet another drain on my sisters and me, who were expected to go along with this fiasco. I had had it. I clearly laid out to him why this choice to remarry so quickly was unreasonable, insensitive and, most importantly, why I would be having no part of it.

It's really difficult to explain to people who have "normal" families what this is like. And at this point I don't really feel I have to explain myself to anyone, as much as I need to save myself and my son. When I told my dad I no longer wanted him in my life and listed the reasons why, much along the lines of the things I mention in this chapter, he replied, "Friendship is a two way street." I was dumbfounded. For one thing he was supposed to be my father, not my friend, for another I realized that he would never take responsibility for his part in anything. It was always everyone else's fault. I realized that my dad saw himself as a victim and someone to whom things just happened, instead of someone who could make choices and decisions that would change his life for the better. Unfortunately, when someone blames everyone else for their problems, then they are helpless to change themselves or take steps to change what is happening in their life. He didn't understand what it was to be a father, as he had never been my father in the traditional sense anyway.

Growing up in my family always felt like being on a tour bus with a crazy driver, who was speeding towards a cliff. There were moments of fun and adventure, art and leisure, and brief moments when we came together around the dinner table or on vacation. Yet, all too often, I would be screaming, "Wait! Stop! Watch out!" Flailing my arms, trying to catch my parents' attention, knowing that they would never listen to me. Whatever I did, it would never be enough. Whatever I said, they would ignore me. I could never save them from themselves or each other. Ultimately, the only thing I could do was to yank open the escape hatch and jump clear.

How to Forgive?

I know that I'm not alone.

We have all been betrayed, abandoned, left standing in the proverbial cold, beaten down and heartbroken by at least one person at some point in our lives. We must allow ourselves to feel our anger, acknowledge our disappointments and mourn our losses *before* moving on.

A friend said to me over brunch one day, "You have to let this go." But I wondered, *Is that more for my benefit or his?* My anger was making him feel uncomfortable. It was so unlike me. I was usually the one cheering him up. I was raw, intense and scary. My rage brought up his own issues. I told him, "Yes, I will…but not today." Another friend couldn't handle my fury at all. It brought up her own discomfort with her own anger at her relatives. She disappeared from my life not long afterwards, and I accepted that I could confide in some people and not in others. Ironically, my male friends were better able to handle my pain than most of the females. Women are trained to be pleasant and non-confrontational.

We live in a culture in which people expect instant gratification, fast food and sitcom-style resolutions. Life isn't like that. It takes some time to heal. If we plan to continue a relationship with another person, we must talk about the difficult issues with them. If they can't or won't acknowledge us, we need to decide whether it is worth being involved with that person and to what degree. Research in "The Doormat Effect: When Forgiveness Erodes Self-Respect and Self-Concept Clarity" by Luchies, Finkel, McNulty and Kumashiro in 2010 revealed that "…feeling like you always have to forgive your partner may end up lowering your feelings of self-respect over time."[24] This is likely true of most relationships, not just romantic partnerships. Research has shown that forgiveness is good overall, but forgive the wrong person too many times without consequences for his/her poor behavior, and you end up feeling badly about yourself.

That said, I really don't want to dwell on the past or feel sorry for myself, blaming myself, my ex-husband or my parents for their mistakes, doomed to remain bitter. I want to be a better partner and parent, knowing that I will likely make my own share of stupid mistakes, for which my own son will one day hold me accountable. I want to be forgiven, too. I choose to be happy. By that I mean I want to be grateful that I survived my crazy childhood and adolescence and that I still have a loving friendship with my ex-husband and co-parent. I want to appreciate that I have many friends who are like a family to me. I want to be able to feel everything, yet not remain stuck in the negative. I want to choose to laugh, be lighthearted, caring and loving, free to pursue the activities that delight me and others. I want to be able to support others in their own growth and choices to make their own lives better, regardless of the circumstances of their birth and upbringing.

My Aunt Amy told me over the phone, "I'm very sorry. I acknowledge your pain." Then she told me that when my dad was a baby, he had several febrile seizures, and that growing up he seemed to work harder than his siblings to excel in school. "But you should talk to Linda," she said, "because I was the youngest, much younger than they, and didn't really know the older kids. I was like an only child." As fate would have it, my Aunt Linda, the eldest sister, was in town. When we spoke on the phone, she told me, "I disagree that there is anything wrong with your father mentally or physically, but I also had a difficult time forgiving my own father, your grandfather. I was bitter for 50 years." I was surprised. I hadn't known she had felt that way for so long. She continued, "You know the saying, 'To err is human, to forgive is divine?' What finally helped was prayer, the laying on of hands by my friends and God's Divine intervention. It was a miracle." Even though I am Interfaith, not

Christian, I asked my aunt to pray for me and my father, as well as the rest of the family.

Being a life coach and writer, I also turned to research to find a way through. According to Dr. Fred Luskin in his groundbreaking book, *Forgive for Good: A Prescription for Health and Happiness*, it is possible and helpful to practice forgiveness daily:

> **Guided Practice of the HEAL Method (Full Version)**
> 1) Think of an unresolved grievance in your life. Pick one where you can at least imagine you could feel different.
> 2) Practice Heart Focus for three to five minutes. Focus your attention in the area around your heart. Ensure that you are breathing slowly and deeply into and out of your belly.
> 3) Reflect for a moment on what you would have preferred to happen in this specific situation. Make an *H* statement to reflect your *Hope* that is personal, specific and positive.
> 4) Hold in your heart in your H statement: "I hoped…"
> 5) When the *H* statement is clear, then *Educate* yourself about the limitations in demanding things always work out the way you want. Make your *E* statement broad and in your heart understand and accept that you are okay even though all your hopes cannot be gratified.
> 6) *Affirm* your positive intention (*A*), the positive long-term goal underneath the hope you had for this specific situation.
> 7) With determination, hold your *A* statement in the warm feelings in your heart. Repeat your positive intention a couple of times.
> 8) Make an L statement, which stands for a Long-Term Commitment to
>   - Practice the HEAL method;
>   - Follow your positive intention even when difficult;
>   - Learn the skills you need to manifest your positive intention;
>   - Practice each letter in order at least twice.

9) Then continue to breathe slowly and deeply into and out of your belly for another thirty seconds to a minute…

To get optimal benefit from the HEAL method, practice the full version at least once each day. The benefits are great if at first you practice twice each day. I advise all people to practice the full method at least once every day for a week.[25]

This technique is the best of the many I have read about in books on active forgiveness. I believe it works because it focuses not only on the grievance to be healed, but also on our thoughts about it and the unresolved pain around the hope that was lost in the process of a betrayal. It uses body and breath awareness, as well as awareness of thoughts and a resolution to continue to refocus attention on the intention to forgive. In other words Dr. Luskin's HEAL method connects all parts of ourselves, body-heart-mind-spirit, to resolve the deep hurt that is always underneath the anger. It also allows the forgiver to recommit each time the pain returns, and it will return often, to moving beyond the transgression and to choose to heal.

In Hawaiian culture there is a practice known as *ho'oponopono*. This practice is very similar to Dr. Luskin's HEAL method in that it requires the forgiver to recall the transgression and notice how it impacts him or her, as well as to reconcile and release it. Yet *ho'oponopono* also includes a spiritual perspective and interconnected worldview about how unforgiveness may cause illness and dis-ease. According to Pukui's and Elbert's *Hawaiian Dictionary*, *ho'oponopono* is defined as "mental cleansing: family conferences in which relationships were set right through prayer, discussion, confession, repentance and mutual restitution and forgiveness."[26] People were not expected to "go it alone," as we so often do in America and the West. Families and communities lived in harmony and worked actively to create it. We are interconnected.

Ho'oponopono in modern times is taught in a variety of ways by a variety of practitioners. In essence it comes down to five simple phrases that are easy to say but not always so easy to mean: "I'm sorry. Please forgive me. I forgive you. Thank you. I love you." My Aunt Sue wrote via e-mail, "It has been an extremely painful time for you. I am very proud of all that you have accomplished in your short life and know that you deserve all the success that comes to you." *Ho'oponopono* is about taking full responsibility for our lives and actions. By forgiving another, we forgive ourselves. By forgiving ourselves, we forgive the others.

Honor yourself and others enough to allow the process of feeling challenging emotions, releasing them over and over again and working your way through them. In the New Testament of the Bible, Jesus is reported to have taught the following:

> Then Peter came to Jesus and asked, "Lord, how many times shall I forgive my brother when he sins against me? Up to seven times?"
>
> Jesus answered, "I tell you, not seven times, but seventy-seven times." Matthew 18:21-22

Forgiveness may take many, many attempts before it is possible to let go. It depends upon the people involved, the circumstances of the transgression and the depth of the injury. For me it has taken much more than seventy-seven times. I've lost count.

However, forgiveness is not forgetting. It does not mean that what someone else did or said is right. It does not mean that they are allowed to hurt you or to cause you any harm again. Forgiveness is remembering who we really are and who we want to become. Forgiveness allows us to move forward in our lives. We actively choose to leave the past behind us, so we can be fully present and create a better future. Forgiveness allows love to exist. In forgiveness we are finally free.

Forgiveness Explorations:

If you have 5 to 10 minutes, answer the following:

Have you forgiven others for events in the past? If not, why not?

Have you forgiven yourself? If not, why not?

For what have you been forgiven?

Do you believe certain actions are unforgivable? If so, why? What are these, specifically? Is it possible that anything is forgivable, even if not forgettable?

If you have more time, answer the following:

Is there something in your past that still needs to be healed, brought to the light or made whole? If so, what is it?

Do you tend to resolve difficult situations as they arise in your life or to take more time to resolve them?

Think about what you can do to forgive yourself (or another). Do you need to ask for forgiveness, to make amends somehow and/or just to move on?

Self Love

Everything has its beauty, but not everyone sees it.
—Confucius

The Greatest Love of All

When we hear the term "self-love," some of us may cringe, thinking that this means being self-absorbed or New-agey. Or we might wonder if that word means the same thing as self-esteem. Some of us may only recently have gotten to a space of self-like and have become less judgmental of ourselves, or we may still vacillate between self-confidence and self-abuse. I use the word self-love to mean a state of being in which we do not judge ourselves harshly, where we hold ourselves accountable and responsible, but never to blame or shame. In self-love we take care of ourselves as we would our best friends and other loved ones with compassion, kindness and tenderness. In truth, self-love allows us to love others even better. It opens up a generosity and expansiveness of the heart and spirit that self-loathing can never permit. By loving ourselves, we love to the fullest degree possible.

Dr. Kristin Neff, researcher and author of *Self-Compassion: Stop Beating Yourself Up and Leave Insecurity Behind* writes:

> The research that my colleagues and I have conducted over the past decade shows that self-compassion is a powerful way to achieve emotional well-being and contentment in our lives. By giving ourselves unconditional kindness and comfort while embracing the human experience, difficult as it is, we avoid destructive patterns of fear, negativity, and isolation. At the same time, self-compassion fosters

positive mind-states such as happiness and optimism. The nurturing quality of self-compassion allows us to flourish, to appreciate the beauty and richness of life, even in hard times.[27]

By treating ourselves with the same kindness and consideration we show others, we can achieve more balance and peace. Instead of continually putting ourselves down, we can become more productive, interconnected with others and more effective. While we don't sugarcoat anything about life, we are more compassionate towards others when we are self-compassionate, too. Over a decade of psychological research by Dr. Neff and others has shown that self-compassion actually increases optimism, productivity and success, as well as resiliency and the ability to overcome adversity. In fact scientific research in the field of positive psychology has shown that one of the greatest indicators of future success is how resilient we are to failure and how quickly we can make positive meanings of even the most challenging parts of our lives. Self-compassionate people bounce back more quickly when knocked down. Well-being, optimism and success are directly correlated with how loving we are towards ourselves and others.

Children are innately self-compassionate. They rest when they need to, cry for food and drink and make requests for love and nurturing. When did we forget how to care for and love ourselves? Girls learn early that their appearance is the means to power, status and securing a mate. Boys learn that how much money they earn at a job is the key to success. Yet, it's not that we want deliberately to hurt or treat ourselves poorly. It's often just a set of bad habits we developed over time, based on past experiences, such as others' expectations or false beliefs that once had a function but that now no longer serve us. Our culture has several sayings and beliefs that bolster the false attitude that one should be hard on oneself, rather than compassionate: "When the going gets tough, the tough get going," "Suck it up!" or "Don't be a cry baby!" Sometimes it was our family interactions, cultural or religious expectations and beliefs that led us to believe that it is somehow self indulgent or selfish to love ourselves. How ironic, in a culture that believes in individuality, that we somehow view loving self as a bad thing.

My Love Story

I have not always loved who I am. Growing up as a girl in an Asian-American family in Hawai'i in the 1970s and '80s, I was shown that girls were not as important as boys. It wasn't so much through direct statements as much as indications that girls should be quiet, polite and serve the males in the household. I remember my younger sister, Lea, asking my grandmother once, "Why doesn't Grandpa ever make you a sandwich?" She had noticed that Grandma, even though a full-time elementary school teacher, also did the housework and cooking and served my grandfather's meals. My Grandpa Kwon also worked full-time, did yard work and other tasks, but he was not expected to be deferential in quite the same way. "It's a sign of respect," Grandma said, patting her hand and moving her out of the way, so she could get the dishes down from the cupboard. A feminist even at so tender an age, my sister replied, "Doesn't Grandpa also respect you?" My grandmother did not reply, and her face gave no indication of having registered this contradiction.

It was a generational disconnect. Grandpa Kwon would take us kids for chocolate-dipped ice cream at Dairy Queen and let us hang on to him, protecting us from the big waves at the beach. He was the provider and patriarch. My grandmother showed her love through her cooking, buying us presents and by sewing my sisters and me matching dresses each year. However, my sisters and I still would help Grandma and Mom in the kitchen, while Dad and Grandpa could relax and watch T.V. in the next room. I know that if I had been a boy, things would have been different. This was about an unknown word, *privilege*, that I didn't fully understand back then. Cultural, generational and familial expectations were like scripts in a play that everyone in the family performed without even knowing we had memorized them. It was just "the way things are."

In addition to subliminal messages from my family, I also did not match the perceived mainstream notions of external beauty, and I still do not embody the Hollywood or fashion magazine model ideal of beauty. In this day and age beauty means extreme thinness to the point of anorexia. According to Pamela Peeke, MD, MPH, FACP in "Everyday Fitness" on WebMD: "The average starlet is wearing a size 2 or 4 which is the sample size designers are making presently. Today, the average American woman is 5'4", has a waist size of 34-35 inches and weighs between 140-150 lbs, with a dress size of 12-14."[28] Like the average American woman, I am a size 12-14, 5'4", and I weigh slightly more than average. It used to be challenging to look in the mirror and see someone beautiful back when I was in high school in the late '80s. I was insecure and different, though I was also proud of my eccentricity. The saving grace for me was art—drama, writing and photography—as well as having out-of-the-ordinary role models like actors Winona Ryder and Johnny Depp, singers Cyndi Lauper, Dave Gahan of Depeche Mode and Robert Smith of the Cure and comediennes Whoopi Goldberg and Bette Midler.

Like many other American women, I dieted, exercised like crazy and tried spa routines and even painful surgeries. I had cosmetic procedures done, such as vein sclerotherapy to remove varicose veins, brachioplasty and laser liposuction to remove excess fat that couldn't be exercised away. I plucked grey hairs whenever they came in and avoided going to the beach when I wasn't feeling toned and fit. The ironic thing was that, even with these external interventions, I was still me, full of insecurities. Even when others would tell me how fabulous I looked, I didn't believe it, until years later, when I finally accepted my stretch marks and flab, grey hairs and scars along with my innate beauty.

I realized that my body was healthy. It had repeatedly healed from injury, illness and a C-section childbirth, and, quite frankly, it had seen me through life quite well. I began to love my bountiful body for taking such good care of me, and I began to treat it like an ally, instead of an enemy. I began calling myself beautiful and strong and smart and was not so focused on how others might view me. This was a process over several years, and with that shift in perception, I also changed.

It is challenging in an era of supermodels and mass media photoshopped images for some of us to see the natural beauty that exists in each and every person. External beauty fades over time, and we need a more inclusive and realistic standard of beauty that honors each person's character, too. More and more people are waking up to their own inherent beauty and self-worth and the beauty and worth of others.

However, it isn't just external beauty that impacts one's ability to love oneself and others. There is also the subjective and often incorrect self-image we may inflict upon ourselves. Not only did I not have compassion or love for myself as an adolescent, but for a long time I had the false belief that I was worthless, and I worked extra hard as an honor roll student to prove the opposite, that I was worthy and, therefore, lovable. This constant striving allowed for no rest and no latitude for growth or learning. It was exhausting to keep such an unrealistically high standard.

As a young child I had had no doubt of my inherent beauty and right to exist and be happy. However, the childhood sexual assault I experienced and my parents' benign neglect, self-absorption and inability to face this and other problems in their lives were, in large part, responsible for my own loss of natural self-love and healthy self-compassion. It took assertiveness training, critical thinking skills, the accomplishment of many of my goals, the love of a devoted partner and friends and work in service to others before I believed that I am, indeed, enough. It took many years before I realized I was worthy of love, my own or anyone else's.

I still have moments of insecurity and uncertainty, but these are less frequent and less intense. I would not wish the trauma of my past on anyone; yet, I also know it makes me a more empathetic coach and person. We can take our wounds, talents, skills and even our tragedies and make something good come of them. No matter what we face in life, no matter who breaks our hearts or what unexpected events sideswipe us, we can choose the meaning we make of all of it. This includes the meaning we create about ourselves. Therein lies our true power, to love ourselves and others no matter what and to know that we are inherently worthy, that we are good enough just by being us. It is by relaxing into who we are right now, rather than striving to be someone different, that we find self-acceptance, self-compassion and self-love.

The "Pursuit of Happiness," Self-Compassion and Self-Love

Similarly, for many people, especially in America, the "pursuit of happiness" is desirable, but many feel unworthy or unable to enjoy actual happiness in the moment, if and when we do achieve it. According to researcher Caroline Adams Miller,

MAPP and Dr. Michael B. Frisch in *Living Your Best Life: The Ultimate Life List Guide*:

> The connection between pursuing challenging goals and being happier is impossible to deny. We have shown you that happy people are optimistic, believe in their capabilities, and wake up every day with a variety of short-term and long-term goals that engage them and provide meaning, purpose, and pleasure in their lives. Happy people live longer, have more friends, are healthier, persist in their endeavors, and succeed more often in life *because* of their upbeat outlook on life.[29]

There is a strong connection between being happier and optimism, confidence and goal-setting. Happy people have learned that accepting, having compassion for and loving oneself are vitally important. An upbeat outlook on life is also a component in self-love, both of which are possible to learn if we don't already know how to be happy or to love. Research by positive psychologists, including Miller and Neff among several others cited in this book, in the areas of happiness, gratitude, perseverance, self-compassion, personal strengths, altruism and success has shown that it is possible to take steps to change one's life for the better. Miller also includes bucket lists and following through on those lists for a more meaningful life. However, part of that change requires self-acceptance and a willingness to relax into what is and surrender, rather than constantly striving for the next goal.

In fact this kind of self-compassion actually allows for more fulfillment and happiness and for more opportunity for success in life. Research by Dr. Kristin Neff and others has shown that self-compassion actually makes us less likely to hurt ourselves and others. More to the point, there is the false belief that loving ourselves could somehow make us less loving. Loving oneself actually has been shown to make us more loving and accepting towards others, especially our partners. According to Dr. Neff in *Self-Compassion*:

> The results of our study indicated that self-compassionate people *did* in fact have happier and more satisfying romantic relationships than those who lacked self-compassion. This is largely because self-compassionate participants were described by their partners as being more accepting and nonjudgmental than those who lacked self-compassion. Rather than trying to change their partners, self-compassionate people tended to respect their partners' opinions and consider their point of view. They were also described as being more caring, connected, affectionate, intimate, and willing to talk over relationship problems than those who lacked self-compassion. At the same time, self-compassionate men and women were described as giving their partners more freedom and autonomy in their relationships. They tended to encourage partners to make their own decisions and to follow their own interests.[30]

By loving and having compassion for ourselves, we are more secure and interconnected. We can foster positive relationships and deal effectively and honestly with our partners, even when things are not going well in a relationship. When we love ourselves and are compassionate towards ourselves, we are less needy, fearful and less judgmental of others and, therefore, more capable of genuine affection and love for other people. I would also argue that self-compassion and acceptance would naturally extend to other family members and friends. When we are self-compassionate and self-loving, we bring our whole selves to any relationship: healthy, non-judging and authentic selves.

Sensuality is Sacred

Say the word "sensual," and it rolls off the lips and tongue like a kiss. According to the *Oxford Dictionary of Current English*, "sensual" is defined as "relating to the senses as a source of pleasure."[31] Sensuality is about being embodied: touching, smelling, tasting, hearing and seeing. For hundreds of years the body has been considered base or crude and somehow less valuable than the intellect, spirit and heart. Yet the body plays a vital role in living. We must care for our bodies to live fully and well.

Sensuality is sacred.

I have not always had a positive relationship to my body. As I mentioned earlier, like many survivors of sexual assault, I could not fully remember what happened to me for a long time. I put on weight as an adolescent in an unconscious effort to shield and protect my body physically from other people. I was also injured in my late-twenties, and I needed to be fully re-embodied in order to recover. When I was pregnant and gave birth to my son, Noa, at the age of forty, I finally felt like Gaia, the Earth goddess: healthy, sexy and sensual. I enjoyed the way my body could stretch, grow and nurture. I realized it had held me my entire life and asked only that I care for and about it. It was then I began to love my body and revel in my senses.

During that process of remembering and recovering my body, I discovered several practices along the way that supported me in living more sensually in my body. You can try some of these or invent your own:

1) Notice your breath. Breathe in deeply and then out until all the air is gone from your lungs. We rarely breathe deeply. Inhale and notice how invigorated you feel. Do this for several breaths.
2) Touch your skin. Notice how warm or cold it is to the touch. Notice how smooth or rough. Notice how good it feels to be in your own body. (Note: Even if you are experiencing discomfort or pain somewhere in your

body, notice how other areas of your body are feeling. Contrast those sensations.)
3) Take time to smell the flowers, literally. Or good food. Or another scent you love. Breathe so deeply that you can taste the aroma.
4) Taste something salty, sweet or sour. Roll the food around on your tongue and savor it, then swallow. Notice our senses come alive when we pay attention.
5) Listen. Sit still for a moment and notice all of the sounds around you. What does this new awareness bring to you?
6) Close your eyes. Allow them to rest for a second, and then when you open them, notice what you see around you. Are your surroundings pleasant or unpleasant? Do they uplift or depress you? What can you do to change your surroundings to enhance the sense of sight?
7) Get a check up at the doctor, chiropractor, dentist or other healthcare or healing practitioner.
8) Try something new with your body. Enroll in a class that brings awareness to your body. Try various forms of Yoga, Pilates, Gyrotonics, Nia, Feldkenkrais, T'ai Chi, dance, kickboxing, aerobics or some other form physical activity that awakens your senses and makes your body feel good!
9) Get a massage or facial or manicure or pedicure. Take your time with your lover and embrace the senses. Be embodied in the pleasure potential of your senses.
10) Love your body and treat it as if it is your best friend. Be good to your senses.

Newfield Network's Body-Emotion-Language (B-E-L), Observer-Action-Result (O-A-R) Models and Body Dispositions

During my Newfield Network coach training I learned how the body is interconnected with the emotions and language. In Newfield Network terminology, this was known as the "BEL (body-emotion-language) model." I experienced firsthand how holding my body in a particular way allowed certain emotions to arise, such as fear or courage, and discouraged other possibilities. I noticed how my words and thoughts would align with my body posture (what Newfield Network calls the "coherency" of an observer's experiences), accordingly with emotions (short term and changing) and moods (longer term and more closely linked to a state of being). I also noticed and became aware through movement, dance and modeling, guided and taught by Veronica Olalla Love and Josephina Santiago, how I could later shift my thoughts, language and feelings when I shifted my body and when I honored my body. I could center whenever I needed to be calm and present. I could take certain other "body dispositions," such as stability, resolution, flexibility or openness, and experience different states of being, feeling and connection with myself that I had never before encountered in quite the same way. I could view my experience from a different perspective. There was a shift in my awareness as an observer. I could now fully understand what Newfield Network teachers, Daniel Newby and Julio Olalla, meant when they described the "OAR (observer-action-result) model." There were possibilities open to me that did not exist prior to this exercise. In order to change my life from the inside out, it was necessary to become aware of my beliefs and to transform the observer I am. I later took this new perspective and these innovative techniques into my coaching practice in work and play with clients. It was an empowering and deeply moving experience.[32]

Research about "Power Positions" and Hormones like Cortisol and Testosterone

Later, I came across scientific research that has been done recently, proving how intricately linked the body, the production of hormones and the ability to feel and speak actually are. In a TED talk online, social psychologist, researcher and professor at Harvard Business School Amy Cuddy, Ph.D., explains how she and her colleagues, Dana Carney and Andy Yap, were interested in studying whether or not taking on particular nonverbal body postures could alter the levels of testosterone and cortisol in the brains of volunteer test subjects. First they took saliva samples, and then they had subjects take on two submissive or two dominant poses for just one minute each and engage in a risk-taking by gambling, then took saliva samples again. In that short time there was significant change in the level of cortisol (the stress hormone) and testosterone (the dominance hormone). The people posing in submissive positions (curled in or drooping down) had heightened levels of coritsol and lowered testosterone, while the power posers (standing like Wonder Woman or sitting in a king-like pose) experienced the opposite effect. Nonverbal body positions not only impacted how others viewed the test subjects but also how those people felt about themselves. Those in dominant poses were more likely to take risks, and those in submissive poses were more likely to be risk-averse. This led Professor Cuddy to conclude, "Our bodies change our minds, and our minds can change our behavior, and our behavior can change our outcomes" and to advise people: "Don't fake it till you make it. Fake it till you become it."[33]

Sensuality is not only sacred; it is essential to living an empowered life. When we are aware of, awake to our senses and embodied in our bodies, our emotions and words align, and we can make wiser, more positive choices that will impact us and others around us. It, therefore, becomes vital that we invest time and energy in caring for our bodies and learn as much as possible how to align our body positions, thoughts and beliefs, emotions and actions.

Love your body. Love yourself.

"Fiction is obliged to stick to possibilities. Truth isn't." –Mark Twain

I'm bi-beautiful.

This is a term I coined in 2011 when I first came out to friends and family. I invented that word in order to remind myself that it is just a label and that I have the right to wear it as I please and, sometimes, to put it away and focus on other aspects of who I am: mother, entrepreneur, friend, coach, change agent.

From my earliest memories, I have always been attracted to both males and females. I am especially attracted to people who are kind, loving, funny, intelligent and artistic, regardless of their gender. However, societal pressure to be straight was especially "Just Say No" in the '80s and '90s when I grew up. Before I had even been with my first boyfriend, I knew I was different, and I sensed I would not be accepted. My first crushes included Shaun Cassidy, Scott Baio, Molly Ringwald, Sting, Winona Ryder, David Bowie, Dave Gahan, Cyndi Lauper and Johnny Depp. I dated men throughout high school and college, then I met Justin, and we were happily married for nineteen years. We are still best friends.

There are many misconceptions in mainstream heterosexual

culture, as well as among lesbian and gay people, about bi-beautiful people. There is the assumption that we are oversexed, confused or just "want it all." The truth is that many of us are monogamous or in open relationships that are loving, respectful and honest. According to an August 2012 article, "Bisexuality Myths Debunked By Science," by Samantha Joel, M.A. on *The Science of Relationships* website:

> In reality, a great many bisexual individuals have happily monogamous relationships with their partners; for example, by the end of Dr. Diamond's ten-year study, fully 89% of bisexual women were in monogamous, long-term relationships. Furthermore, for those bisexual individuals who do desire multiple sexual partners, research suggests that they typically achieve this goal by negotiating open relationships with their partners, NOT by sneaking around behind their partners' backs.[34]

It is empowering to discover that research confirms that many bi-women like myself prefer committed, monogamous relationships. However, I do not feel that I or anyone else has a right to impose that lifestyle or any other choice on others. Some people also now choose polyamorous relationships with the full consent of their primary partners. Since the famous 1940s Kinsey and 1960s Masters and Johnson research studies into sex and gender, there has been ongoing scientific research done in the areas of sexuality, identity and relationships that includes a wide spectrum of what is considered to be "normal."

According to research in the *National Survey on Family Growth (NSFG)*, which was conducted between 2006 to 2008 and included ~13,500 survey respondents between the ages of 15 to 44 from across the United States:

> 83% of women were attracted only to men, slightly less than 1% were attracted only to women, and 15% expressed some level of attraction to both sexes; 94% of women self-

identify as heterosexual, 1% as homosexual and 4% as bi-sexual.

94% of men were attracted only to women, slightly more than 1% were attracted only to men, and 5% expressed some level of attraction to both sexes; 96% of men self-identify as heterosexual, 2% as homosexual/gay, and 1% as bisexual.[35]

While these percentages are self-reported, and it is likely that today's LGBTQ numbers are actually higher, it still provides an intriguing snapshot of scientific research on attraction, as compared with self-labeled sexual identity. 15% of women attracted to both sexes, but only 4% self-identifying as bi-sexual? 5% of men expressing attraction to both sexes, but only 1% self-identifying as bi-sexual? *The Science of Relationships: Answers to Your Questions About Dating, Marriage, and Family* offers this and many more intriguing questions and answers.

Truthfully, being bi- is a beautiful part of who I am. I love people, though not all of them physically; and, unless I'm planning on sleeping with you, you likely really don't care. I've noticed that the people who do get upset about it are wrestling with their own demons, doctrines and dichotomies. Yet, it is inspiring to be part of a rising group of "rainbow people," who are choosing to be true to ourselves by embracing relationships that are in integrity with who we are.

I debated coming out in this way, because there are political and social, professional and personal ramifications. Interestingly, most of my straight friends recommended *not* coming out. They said that "it didn't matter" in a book such as this. Most of my LGBTQ friends said to be honest with myself and others, that it would have a lasting loving impact for others who debate coming out fully. All of my friends love me no matter what. Yet, it is important to point out certain biases and privileges.

Straight people never have to ask themselves, *Should I tell them I'm straight or not?*, nor do they have to be afraid that they will be rejected or scorned or thrown out because of a core part of who they are. The assumption among mainstream Americans is that being heterosexual is the norm. Also, people who discover I am bi-, and not straight, seem to feel like I lied to them or betrayed them in some way, especially straight women. Straight people seem to view bi-beautiful people like we are wolves in sheep's clothing, while gay and lesbian people sometimes think bi-beautiful people can "pass" as heterosexual and, therefore, have it easier than they do. A friend of mine explained to me that "politically and socially gays and lesbians are trying to fit into mainstream by asserting that being gay is not a choice but a natural part of who they are, and being bi-sexual seems to contradict that." In truth being bi-beautiful is also a natural way of being and not a choice.

Bi-sexuals have likely existed for as long as mankind has walked the Earth. Notable historical figures as Alexander the Great, Hadrian, Julius Caesar, William Shakespeare, D.H. Lawrence, Virginia Woolf, Frida Kahlo, up to David Bowie, Madonna and Lady Gaga, are included among three hundred fifty others in an illustrious list, "Famous Bisexual People in History," compiled by Sheela Lambert, founder of the Bi Writers Association and its Bisexual Book Awards and *Bi Lines* reading series.[36]

I am choosing to come out, if for no other reason, than that it is important to me to be authentic. I choose to be me: Hapa, Interfaith, Bi-beautiful and any other label I choose or decline to be.

Love Manifest

Thus, it was not until I was 43 that I finally came to understand that I couldn't expect to find the "right" someone, the ideal job or even lose that last ten pounds so that everything else in my life would then be "perfect." Instead I knew that I had to find the rightness, ideal and perfection in myself right in every moment and discover that it was there all along. I had to embrace, not push away, all of who I was, including my dark, sad and scary parts. I also knew that I was capable of making choices that were healthy, wise and fun.

When seeking self-acceptance and love, remember it is already within us, though it may take practice to discover, uncover and recover. Based on my own experiences with rediscovering love and compassion for myself, I recommend the following:

1) Ask yourself what you would say or do for your best friend in the same circumstances, then say or do that for yourself.
2) Hang out only with people who uplift and inspire you and avoid critical, insensitive types.
3) Treat yourself to one special thing a day. This could be time to rest or a piece of chocolate or another small treat or doing something you love to do, because you deserve it.
4) Wear clothes and shoes that you like and which fit you properly and make you feel good about yourself.
5) Participate in activities and groups that accentuate your talents and strengths.
6) Keep only the gifts, objects and keepsakes that hold meaning and good memories for you.
7) Connect with others who have integrity, and be honest with yourself about what motivates your interest in others.

8) Say "No" to things, people and events out of alignment with who you are. When you say "Yes!" only to things, people and events that resonate as true for you, then you say "Yes!" to your highest Self, to those in alignment with you and to Spirit.

And, finally
9) Ask and reach out for support from trusted friends, colleagues and mentors whom you admire.

Aligning Thoughts, Words and Actions

Self-love requires aligning one's thoughts, words and actions. Sometimes people believe that things are the way they are and that we can't change them. "You can't teach an old dog new tricks," goes the old saying. But, in actuality, we can learn healthier and better ways to approach our problems, goals and day-to-day lives. First of all, we have to be aware of what our limiting and false beliefs are. Some steps I have found helpful when working with clients' false beliefs:

1) First of all, notice how your body feels when you think these thoughts. Does your heart constrict or open? Does your stomach clench or relax? Are your shoulders up to your ears or loose and comfortable? Change the position in which you are standing, sitting or lying down, and notice if the thought or belief also changes.
2) Note the exceptions and moments when a particular belief or thought is not true and the pieces of the puzzle don't fit together. Notice the dissonance and chaos and stay present with it when it occurs.
3) Breathe. Notice the breath whenever caught up in thoughts or feelings. By breathing deeply, we can modulate our physical sensations, feelings and thoughts, becoming calmer, clearer and more self-aware. It is in

these moments, in clarity, awareness and openness, that we can notice our thoughts, beliefs and feelings and see them pass through us or notice how they latch onto us.

It is in times of transition, transformation and transcendence that we find the gateway to something better and more authentic, self-acceptance, self-compassion and self-love.

Self-Love Explorations:

If you have 5 to 10 minutes, answer the following:

What are some of the stories you tell yourself about you? How do you tend to identify yourself? Considering these, are they accurate and fairly objective or relentlessly negative and subjective?

What are a few ways you can be more loving towards yourself? For example, do you tell and show yourself acceptance, compassion and love every day?

If not, why not? Is/Are there (an) event(s) that occurred that you haven't yet come to terms with in your life?

If so, make a list of the actions you already do and add one or two more ideas.

What are a couple of ways that you can change your beliefs so that they are more self-compassionate?

If you have more time:

At my 25th high school reunion in 2012, I had the chance to reconnect with several high school friends, including some of my dearest and closest friends. It was one of those moments when one has a chance to look back at who we all were and who we have become and to reassess who we want to be now. I was surprised when they told me that they remembered me as a "cool" kid and one of the "in-crowd." I had always thought of myself as an observer bordering on outsider, able to move effortlessly from group-to-group, but never really a part of any. I was friendly and kind and I still am, but I never thought of myself as cool or popular.

Perhaps your memories of yourself are likewise skewed? Perhaps it would be worth reconnecting with an old friend to gain some perspective on who you were then and who you are and want to be now? Develop some questions to ask this person, then, if you are ready, e-mail, call or message them to get their point of view.

Transcendence

*Never doubt that a small group of thoughtful,
committed, citizens can change the world.
Indeed, it is the only thing that ever has.*
–Margaret Mead

Pain is a Necessary Part of Growth

Ironically, it was because of the most painful moments of my life that I began to find worth in all parts of myself, including the "negative" or "bad" parts. Pain is a necessary part of growth, but I don't have to remain stuck. As I once wrote to a good friend of mine, "Who better to write a book on empowerment, interconnection and hope than someone who was once so badly out of balance that she almost took herself out of the picture?"

It is still a sometimes painful and challenging process, but in uncovering and exposing memories and feelings to the light, I have found a truer sense of my purpose and worth. I have found value beyond the paycheck I bring home or the roles I take on when I am with others. I can feel everything, and I have found an essential Self that is always there, a central core of strength that I draw upon when everything else in my life goes to hell. It is the difference between living a life weighed down by others' expectations and beliefs and living an authentic life for which I am responsible and accountable. I am living my life mission.

I would like to be able to say that there was a continuous upward progression, but, in fact, there were a couple of slip-ups and setbacks with my addictions and the need to reassess my balance from time to time. I understood that I could choose to use all of my experiences to make a positive difference in my own life and in the lives of others, or I could remain stuck in self-pity, blame and regret, which would benefit no one.

The Potential to Make Better Choices and Live a Better Life

As a transitions life coach, I believe in each person's potential to make better choices and live a better life. While there are not excuses for poor choices, and all actions have consequences and outcomes, there are always underlying reasons for our actions. No matter what the situation, we still have a choice about how we interpret it and what we make of it in our lives. What is important is that we speak our truths. None of us can change the past, but we can make better choices in the present and future. Who we are really depends upon who we *believe* we are, based upon the sum total of all our life choices and experiences, tragedies and triumphs. I now believe that the integration of all parts of the Self and maintaining balance over time are the keys to healing ourselves and encouraging others to heal, as well. I believe in transcendence.

Each of Us Must Awaken

With the state of the world the way it is now, we can't wait around for our leaders to show the way. We can't wait for another Martin Luther King, Jr. or even another Gandhi, Mother Teresa or Nelson Mandela. We can't afford to remain stuck in self-pity and regret about the past or in worry and anxiety about the future. Each of us must awaken to whatever it is we are here to do—and do it now with love, joy and a sense of purpose. Then we can choose to join with others on similar missions, with similar goals, to improve the world.

Some questions to consider when at a crossroads:

1) What is my intention in taking this action?
2) Will I and/or others be impacted positively or negatively?
3) Will this action enhance or diminish us all?
4) Am I certain that what I think is true is actually true when I take this action?
5) How will my action be interconnected to other people's actions? In other words, will my action cause a chain reaction of events that will move forward in a positive or negative direction? Today, tomorrow and far into the future....

Embrace WE-thinking instead of ME-thinking

In this time of political and social upheaval—with the June 2013 voiding of section four of the Voting Rights Act, the poisoning of our food supply with insecticides and GMOs and other damage being done to the environment, as well as the continued assault on our freedoms, privacy and civil rights—it's time to work actively towards harmonious win-win outcomes for all concerned and to embrace WE-thinking instead of ME-thinking. It is up to us to vote, sign petitions, march and protest peacefully and spend money on goods and services in alignment with our values.[37]

Create CoPOWERment

We must think beyond our personal or professional interests, and even our national interests, and care about all beings with whom we are interconnected and with whom we share this planet. We can choose to join with organizations that protect, uphold and embody our values. When we recognize we are interconnected with other beings—including plants, insects, animals—only then will we respect the impact we have upon them and they upon us. When we consider our thoughts, words and actions in relation to how they impact all concerned, only then can we mindfully and actively create coPOWERment.

Certification in the Creating CoPOWERment® Coaching Techniques will be available in 2014

Creating CoPOWERment® Workshops currently available:
Setting Intention, Choosing Priorities & Visualizing Goals© incorporates a priorities exploration, vision collage and other inspiring and fun activities in an interactive, small group session to transform your life for the better.

Emotional Balance, Mindful Movement & Relaxation© utilizes an emotional balance exploration, mindful movements and relaxation techniques in a hands-on, small group session.

Community CoPOWERment© focuses on aligning participants with like-minded/hearted/souled communities, using fun, interactive exercises and community resources in a small group session.

One-on-One Creating CoPOWERment® Professional Coaching Worldwide:
Seeking tailor-made coaching for goal-setting, action-planning, visualizing the future, actively moving step-by-step towards win/win solutions?

Lani specializes in short term (3- to 6-month) life redesign, before, during and after life transitions such as graduation, moving, career change, marriage, new baby, divorce, retirement, coming out, recovery, etc.…

International coaching one-on-one in-person, by phone, e-mail and/or videoconferencing available by appointment.

Contact lani@coPOWERment.com for more information.
www.coPOWERment.com

Acknowledgements

Much aloha (love) and mahalo nui loa (thanks so much) to the people listed below:

To those who shared their transformational stories with me in interviews and who were willing to share them with you: Master Wasentha Young, Sifu Greg Knollmeyer, Kellie Carbone, Sura Dahn Kim, Janis Paul, Dan/Pearl Dynasty, Martina Ashanti, Amy B. Garber, Gina Fedock-Robinson, Dr. Arash Babaoff and Michael Purcell.

To those who have written blurbs and endorsements, including Karen Davis, Patricia Fero, Mary Anne Flanagan, Clayton Gibson, Daniel Newby, Jim Smith, Jayne Warrilow and Master Wasentha Young. Special thanks to Master Coach and Newfield Network founder, Julio Olalla, for writing the foreword to this book and his continued support and encouragement.

To my former writers' group in Honolulu, Hawai'i the aptly named *Coolest Writing Group Ever Meet Up*, first organized by Dominic Pileri in 2010 and consisting of ~20 writers, including: Dan Baram, Joanna Bressler, Hiyaguha Cohen, Jonella DeLimas, Natasha Fisher, Paul Franco, Lisa Gollin, Kilei Nelson, Patty Palmer, Dominic and Nicole Pileri, Laura Rayburn, Ralph Saint Romain, Erin Shishido, Tyla Smith, Ashlyn Venema, Norm Winter, Myrtle Wong, and, last but not least, Alison and Celia Asoka. Special thanks go to the following writers, whose feedback on the entire book manuscript was essential in making this book better: Fred Barnett, Cynthia Christian, Tammy Evrard and Susan Wright. Extra special thanks goes to

Brian Borell for his loving support, suggestions for structuring this book in a more organized way and for suggesting Balboa Press, an imprint of Hay House Inc., to whom I sent the final manuscript.

To the *Goddessy Writers* in Ann Arbor, Michigan, who helped me edit and revise earlier versions of some of these chapters from 2007 to 2010: Kindred Kellie Carbone, Amazing Amy Garber, Wondrous Wasentha Young and Marvelous Magdalena Spiewla-Roddy.

To my mentor coaches, teachers, support staff and colleagues through Newfield Network www.newfieldnetwork.com: Julio Olalla, Daniel Newby, Josephina Santiago, Veronica Love, Carol Shannon, Kara Erlich, Terri MacKenzie, Deanne Prymek, Karen Curnow, Connie MacKinnon, Chris Beauchamp, Bruce Kirschner, José Ignacio Silva, Mariana Sedano, Eliane Alabe DeBlauw, Natalie Turner, Denise Barnes and Monica Lugo, Karen Davis, Kaytura Felix, among the others in my June 2012 graduating class.

To Justin Meilgaard for editing all editions of all the chapters for content, punctuation and grammar, my sisters, Lea Ann Yancey and Laura Sue Anderson, and my aunts, Amy Kamikawa, Linda Quist and Sue Kwon, for their input and memories. Much aloha to Guy-ding Light DeConte for editing "Leaving Baggage Behind" and for being an Earth angel, dear friend and muse to me, to Co-Creator Clayton Gibson for continued friendship, mentoring and editing and publishing "Striking at the Root of Bullying: Healing the Bully Heart" on MyOutSpirit. com and AbFab/Fair Farhad Zamani, my inspirational Star Trek resource and *Imzadi*.

Thanks also go to Marty Oliphant, Executive Director of the National Association of Social Workers Hawaiʻi Chapter, who published "Because You're Important, Too! Five Things You Can Do in Just a Few Minutes Each Day for Self-Care and Empowerment" in their August 2011 newsletter. Also to Ikaika Hussey, publisher of the *Hawai'i Independent*, who published a book review of Sarah Vowell's *Unfamiliar Fishes*, which I wrote in 2011.

Special thanks to all of my English and Art teachers through the years who have helped me learn, grow and understand, and in particular to the following: Calvin and Sherry Abe, S.D. Chun, Dave Langen, Lala Ostermeyer, Gerald Suyama, Arnold Edelstein, Joan Peters, Ann Rayson, Robert Shapard, Valerie Wayne, Roger Whitlock, Margaret Ferguson, Linda Hogan, Marilyn Krysl and Peter Michelson.

Aloha and mahalo nui also to all of those who have supported me and my work over the years: past mentors, colleagues, clients, students and friends, especially Andrew and Kim Arakawa of Prune Copywriting, Andrea Galvin of Aloha Agency, Rich Fahle of Astral Road Media, Zander Renault of ZR Designs, Ryan Egginton of E12 Web Consulting, Jeff Texeira of Hagadone Printing Company and Loke Buckley Neitzel, who took some amazing photos of me and my 'ohana for PR/Marketing; Diana Wrobel, Julia Wrobel, Pilates Professional Hawaii, Cheryl Tamashiro of Power Pilates Plus LLC, Janna Young; Jake Acedo of W Salon, Mālia Halelā and Renée Tillotson of Still and Moving Center; Dr. Tamara Christiansen, DC, Dr. Daniel Cox, DDS, Dr. Sara Warber, MD, Dr. Gary Saito, DC and Gerald Simmons of Saito Chiropractic, Dr. Allison Bachlet, ND, Dr. Gary Au, DDS, Dr. Shim Ching, MD, Keoni Johnson, Julie DeMello, Susan Lovinger, Molly Ann Indura, Catherine Christmas, Rachel Eckenrod, who healed me and helped me to maintain my health; Lori Chaffin of the *Hawaii Wellness Network*, Ganshet Nandoskar and Char Ravelo of *Inspiration*

Magazine, Jodi Lam of Morgan Stanley Smith Barney, Arnel Mejia of First Hawaiian Bank, Worthy Grace and, last but not least, Marilyn St-Pierre, all of whom supported me with their expertise, talents and businesses.

I love you all and I am truly grateful for you in my life.

Endnotes

[1] Seligman, Dr. Martin E.P. *Flourish: A Visionary New Understanding of Happiness and Well-Being.* New York: Free Press, 2011, 159-160. www.authentichappiness.org.

[2] Zimmerman, J.E. *Dictionary of Classical Mythology.* New York: Bantam Books, 1985.

[3] Pukui, Mary Kawena and Samuel H. Elbert. *The Hawaiian Dictionary, Revised and Enlarged Edition.* Honolulu, HI: University of Hawaii Press, 1986, 193.

[4] *The Oxford Dictionary of Current English, 3rd edition.* Oxford, England: Oxford University Press, 2001, 284.

[5] Jung, Carl. "The Symbolic Life." A Seminar Talk for the Guild for Pastoral Psychology, 1939. London, England 30 June 2013. http://www.jung.org/readingcorner.html.

[6] "Get Educated: What is Domestic Violence?" National Domestic Violence Hotline. 31 January 2013 http://www.thehotline.org/get-educated/what-is-domestic-violence/.

[7] Thomas, Katherine Woodward. *Calling in the One: 7 Weeks to Attract the Love of Your Life.* New York: Three Rivers Press, 2004, 77.

[8] Yancey, Lea. "Mom." E-mail to the author. 27 January 2013.

9 *Star Trek.* Season 3, Episode 12. "The Empath." 6 December 1968.

10 *Star Trek: The Next Generation.* Season 6, Episode 3. "Man of the People." 3 October 1992.

11 Seligman, Dr. Martin E.P. *Flourish: A Visionary New Understanding of Happiness and Well-Being.* New York: Free Press, 2011, 205-206.

12 Seligman, Dr. Martin E.P. *Learned Optimism: How to Change Your Mind and Your Life.* New York: Free Press, 1990.

13 White, David Gordon, ed. *Tantra in Practice: Princeton Reading in Religions.* Princeton, NJ: Princeton Press, 2000, 475-477.

14 Brown, Brené, Ph.D., LMSW. *Daring Greatly: How the Courage to Be Vulnerable Transforms the Way We Live, Love, Parent and Lead.* Gotham Books, a member of Penguin Group (USA) Inc., 2012.

15 DeSalvo, Louise. *Writing as a Way of Healing: How Telling Our Stories Transforms Our Lives.* Boston: Beacon Press, 1999.

16 Pipher, Mary. *Writing to Change the World.* New York: Riverhead Books, Penguin Group, 2006.

17 Newfield Network. *The Art and Practice of Coaching (TAPOC) Training.* October 2011 to June 2012. http://www.newfieldnetwork.com.

18 Seligman, Dr. Martin E.P. *Flourish: A Visionary New Understanding of Happiness and Well-Being.* New York: Free Press, 2011, 33.

[19] **Harris, Carla A.** *Expect to Win: 10 Proven Strategies for Thriving in the Workplace.* New York: Plume, Penguin Group, 2010, 101.

[20] **Harris, Carla A.** *Expect to Win: 10 Proven Strategies for Thriving in the Workplace.* New York: Plume, Penguin Group, 2010, 101-102.

[21] **Harris, Carla A.** *Expect to Win: 10 Proven Strategies for Thriving in the Workplace.* New York: Plume, Penguin Group, 2010, 102.

[22] **Hall, Stacey and Jan Brogniez.** *Attracting Perfect Customers: The Power of Strategic Synchronicity.* San Francisco: Berrett-Koehler Publishers, Inc., 2001, 38.

[23] **Mayhar, Ardath.** *The Soul Singer of Tyrnos.* New York: The Borgo Press, an Imprint of Wildside Press LLC, 1981, 2008.

[24] **Luchies, L. B., E. J. Finkel, J. K. McNulty, and M. Kumashiro.** 2010. "The Doormat Effect: When Forgiveness Erodes Self-Respect and Self-Concept Clarity." *Journal of Personality and Social Psychology.* 98: 734-749. Published in Lewandowski, Gary W. Jr., Ph.D., Timothy J. Loving, Ph.D., Benjamin Le, Ph.D. and Marci E.J. Gleason, Ph.D. Editors. *The Science of Relationships: Answers to Your Questions about Dating, Marriage and Family.* Dubuque, Iowa: Kendall Hunt Publishing Co., 2011, 169.

[25] **Luskin, Fred Dr.** *Forgive for Good: A Prescription for Health and Happiness.* San Francisco: Harper San Francisco, 2002, 175-176.

26 Pukui, Mary Kawena and Samuel H. Elbert. *The Hawaiian Dictionary, Revised and Enlarged Edition.* Honolulu, HI: University of Hawaii Press, 1986, 341.

27 Neff, Kristin, Ph.D. *Self-Compassion: Stop Beating Yourself Up and Leave Insecurity Behind.* New York: William Morrow, an Imprint of Harper Collins Publishers, London, England: Hodder and Stoughton, Hachette UK, 2011, 12-13.

28 Peeke, Dr. Pamela, MD, MPH, FACP "Everyday Fitness." 2010. WebMD.com. http://blogs.webmd.com/pamela-peeke-md/2010/01/just-what-is-an-average-womans-size-anymore.html. 2 August 2012.

29 Miller, Caroline Adams, MAPP and Dr. Michael B. Frisch. *Living Your Best Life: The Ultimate Life List Guide.* New York: Sterling, 2009, 220.

30 Neff, Kristin, Ph.D. *Self-Compassion: Stop Beating Yourself Up and Leave Insecurity Behind.* New York: William Morrow, an Imprint of Harper Collins Publishers, London: England: Hodder and Stoughton, Hachette UK, 2011, 229.

31 *The Oxford Dictionary of Current English, 3rd edition.* Oxford, England: Oxford University Press, 2001, 823.

32 Newfield Network. *The Art and Practice of Coaching (TAPOC) Training.* October 2011 to June 2012. http://www.newfieldnetwork.com.

33 Cuddy, Amy, Ph.D. "Your Body Language Shapes Who You Are." June 2012. Posted October 2012. *TED.com.* 20 May 2013. http://www.ted.com/talks/amy_cuddy_your_body_language_shapes_who_you_are.html.

[34] Joel, Samantha M.A. "Bisexuality Myths Debunked By Science." August 2, 2012. *Science of Relationships.com*. 23 May 2013. http://www.scienceofrelationships.com/home/2012/8/2/bisexuality-myths-debunked-by-science.html.

[35] Chandra, A. W.D. Mosher, and C. Copen. 2011. *Sexual Behavior, Sexual Attraction, and Sexual Identity in the United States. Data from the 2006-2008 National Survey of Family Growth.* Retrieved from http://www.cdc.gov/nchs/data/nhsr/nhsr036.pdf. Published in Lewandowski, Gary W. Jr., Ph.D., Timothy J. Loving, Ph.D., Benjamin Le, Ph.D. and Marci E.J. Gleason, Ph.D. Editors. *The Science of Relationships: Answers to Your Questions about Dating, Marriage and Family.* Dubuque, Iowa: Kendall Hunt Publishing Co., 2011, 188.

[36] Lambert, Sheela. "Famous Bisexual People in History." 25 July 2013. http://www.examiner.com/article/famous-bisexuals-history.

[37] Sheahan, Kyra. "List of International Non Profit Organizations." *EHow.com*. 25 July 2013. http://www.ehow.com/info_8000671_list-international-non-profit-organizations.html.

CPSIA information can be obtained at www.ICGtesting.com
Printed in the USA
LVOW06*1548110913

351392LV00002BB/4/P

9 781452 579306